WE TOOK THE STREETS

WE TOOK THE STREETS

FIGHTING FOR LATINO RIGHTS
WITH
THE YOUNG LORDS

MIGUEL "Mickey" MELENDEZ
Foreword by Jose Torres

RUTGERS UNIVERSITY PRESS
NEW BRUNSWICK, NEW JERSEY, AND LONDON

Originally published in hardcover by St. Martin's Press, 2003
First published in paperback by Rutgers University Press, 2005

Library of Congress Cataloging-in-Publication Data

Melendez, Miguel.
    We took the streets : fighting for Latino rights with the Young Lords /
Miguel "Mickey" Melendez ; with a foreword by Jose Torres.
        p.   cm.
    "First published in a cloth edition by St. Martin's Press in 2003"—T.p. verso.
    Includes index.
    ISBN 0-8135-3559-X (pbk. : alk. paper)
    1. Young Lords (Organization)—History.   2. Puerto Ricans—New York (State)—
New York—Politics and government—20th century.   3. Puerto Ricans—New York
(State)—New York—Social conditions—20th century.   4. Puerto Ricans—
New York (State)—New York—Biography.   5. Political activists—New York
(State)—New York—Biography.   6. New York (N.Y.)—Social conditions—
20th century.   7. New York (N.Y.)—Ethnic relations.   8. New York (N.Y.)—
Biography.   I. Title.

F128.9.P85M455 2005
323.1'168729507471'09—dc22   2004050954

A British Cataloging-in-Publication record for this book is available from the
British Library

Manufactured in the United States of America

To Celia, Miguel, and Elena—my family, who taught me how to be generous with little. To my children—Miguel, Amilcar, Haydee, and Ata-Celia—who are teaching me how to be a father.

To Elizabeth, who lives in my heart. To my friend Dylcia Pagan, who spent twenty years in jail so we could continue to be proud Puerto Ricans. To Richie Perez and Vicente "Panamá" Alba, who never left the front lines. To Filiberto Ojeda, shelter and protect him.

To ending the U.S. embargo against Cuba. To the heroic people of Vieques.

To our youth, our future.

Contents

Only those with an open soul . . . those who never close the door to their own humanity in the search for truth will be free.

—**Rubén Blades**

We give our energies to the noblest cause in the world—the struggle for the liberation of the human race.

—**The Young Lords**

Who are we? We are Puerto Ricans. In order to resolve Puerto Rico's political status, we must first understand who we are and our island's history. In order to destroy our nation, they will have to take our lives.

—**Don Pedro Albizu Campos,
after the Ponce Massacre**

Aquí, you salute your flag first . . . Aquí, to be called negrito means to be called LOVE.

—**Pedro Pietri**

Foreword

I'm in my sixties now, and I've seen much of the world: war and murder and injustice, the assassination of leaders, the triumph of some people, the defeat of others. I've been a boxing champion of the world and a columnist for several newspapers. I've lived in a small town and in the greatest city on Earth. Yet the memories and lessons of my childhood in Playa de Ponce, Puerto Rico, remain the most vivid. One image particularly stands out and influenced my idea of what a man should be—the American soldier. Tall, strong, sharp in his uniform, well-armed to fight enemies, that soldier was my hero, my mentor, my superstar.

I had another hero, too: my father, who was young then, strong, a proud black man and a proud Puerto Rican. Andres Torres was a hardworking, decent, and dignified man. He was respected by everyone in Playa de Ponce. He worked from seven to seven, didn't drink or smoke, and was a good provider—a terrific role-model for a boy at a time when poverty still afflicted so many people on our island. And so was Juanita, my white, Puerto Rican mother. She was only four feet, eleven inches tall but exuded strength, character, and humor.

All of us kids knew that a war was raging somewhere in Europe and the Pacific, and the war was being fought by soldiers like the tall, blond, blue-eyed ones we saw on our streets and beaches. We were boys and didn't know about segregation and so we thought that all soldiers were white, which is to say, all heroes were white. There was no television then, but the movies reminded everyone in my barrio that we were surrounded by beings who were smarter, better-looking, stronger, and more generous than anyone on the planet; that they were protecting us from enemies; that they could never lose a war. At the same time, men who looked just like them were always portrayed as the heroes in cowboy films, while one of them, Tarzan, was even established as king of the African jungle. In Tarzan's world, blacks were either cruel, cowardly, or dumb. It seemed Caucasians were champions everywhere.

The losers always looked like me or my father, my neighbors, my brothers and sisters, my people. The white guys entered a battle and when it was over, there were dead Indians all over the place. Oftentimes, the enemy spoke a "foreign" language, including Spanish. The message, unintended though it may have been, was clear: if you want to be a winner, be like those American soldiers. I promised my ten-year-old pals that in another few years I, too, would don a khaki or blue or white uniform. I would become one of them!

That was the dream of every young man in my generation, and not only in Puerto Rico. No one ever explained to me why we felt that way until almost three decades later. That's when, in the late sixties and early seventies, a group calling itself The Young Lords Organization surfaced in El Barrio, New York. Its members were mostly Puerto Rican, raised on the mainland, or "the States." Most spoke some Spanish, often with difficulty. None, however, showed the docility or submissiveness which too often marked the Puerto Rican personality (only cops, soldiers, outlaws, or prizefighters were allowed to be tough and brave among my people back home). The Young Lords seemed to emerge out of the air itself.

I saw them first on television, then went to visit them in the streets of El Barrio. They were a wonderful group, and I remember meeting Felipe Luciano, Juan González, Denise Oliver, Iris Morales, Pablo "Yoruba" Guzmán, Myrna Martínez, Marlene Cintrón, and Mickey Melendez. They were children of the television era, city people, formally better-educated than I'd ever been. They were evolving theories about what was then called "the underclass" and how its members could be helped to live better, richer lives. Listening to them, sensing their intelligence and idealism, the boundaries of my own view of the world broke open. Mind you, this happened long after I had tasted what was then called the American Dream. I became the world's light heavyweight boxing champion in 1965. I'd walked the streets of the United States, feeling with pride the adulation of all Americans, of all races. I had campaigned at the side of important politicians. I had become the first Puerto Rican to write a column for a "mainstream" American newspaper.

But in the company of the Lords, I realized that in some ways I was still simply a super-spic. I could transcend skin color, language, ethnicity, education, and class barriers that in those years separated Latinos from the ruling class for one simple reason: I was a performer. I was a kind of celebrity, and Americans love celebrities. Winning a boxing crown made me, if only for awhile, an authentic American.

Mingling with the Young Lords brought me much closer to myself as a Latino and as a Puerto Rican. The group made me conscious of the important role that childhood conditions had played in my development as a prizefighter and as a human being. The Young Lords opened new doors. Most were what Aldous Huxley called "the doors of perception." My sense of history and of myself was completely altered. I was not alone. We began to understand what had happened to our island when the Americans arrived with their guns in 1898. We came to realize that colonialism was not just an economic system, but a system that affected every fiber of our consciousness. In the company of the Lords, other questions arose: Was Christopher Columbus a great man because he "discovered" the "new world"? Why didn't we study it from the opposite point of view? What happened when the Tainos and Caribes discovered Columbus or his armed men? Should we as Puerto Ricans be absolutely proud of Juan Ponce de León because he founded the oldest city in the United States, St. Augustine, Florida? Or gave his name to the town where I was born? Or should we have a healthy skepticism about the myths we acquired as children? What was true about our history? What was consoling myth?

The Young Lords taught many of us that history is a series of conflicts. They said that Columbus and Ponce de León tried to exterminate the Indian population they found in the "New World" because they would not work for the newcomers. When guns and disease wasted the native populations (not simply in Puerto Rico, but in Mexico and Peru and other outposts of the colonies) they imported slaves from Africa. The Lords told their version of that history and emphasized that all "truths" were subject to debate.

All of this had a practical side, too. The Young Lords provoked New York's government officials to take a closer look at
lead poisoning among Latino and Black children in poor areas
and persuaded them to do something about it. They forced
school boards in New York City to include Puerto Rican and
Latino history in their curricula. They also compelled local
newspapers to run more commendable stories of Latino life as
alternatives to their usual images of the Puerto Rican-man-in-
handcuffs-slouching-into-jail. The Young Lords were to Puerto
Ricans and other Latinos, what Muhammad Ali was to boxing
and African-Americans: something new and refreshing. This was
an era when the war in Vietnam was infuriating the world (including millions of Americans), but also a time when a wave of
paranoid violence was beginning. The United States, fearful of
the "contagion" of Fidel Castro's communist Cuba, was spon-
soring invasions in the Dominican Republic, (and later) Grenada
and Nicaragua, while at home dissident students were shot for
protesting the violence.

For many Puerto Ricans, the Sixties, which began with the
John F. Kennedy assassination in November 1963, came to a
head with the birth of the Young Lords in July 1969.

The determination and courage shown by the Young Lords,
many of them still in their late teens, on the streets of the South
Bronx, East Harlem, and Brooklyn, encouraged many others to
challenge the sad status quo. If conditions were limiting our opportunities, or shortening our lives, the Young Lords told us that
the situation would change only if we fought back. At the height
of their influence, the Young Lords were the most effective voice
for Latino empowerment in America. They led the way with
great vigor, passion, and intelligence. In my own life, I felt the
old colonial mentality, whose most pernicious aspect is servility,

begin to fade through the influence of their extraordinary collective will.

This book was written by my good friend, Mickey Melendez. Over the years, we remained close, and this is his version of the impact and importance of those years. I don't agree with all of his analysis, but I respect the man and his lifetime of struggle. Mickey helped to organize the "militant" Young Lords while knowing that the most important muscle of all is the mind. Only through its exercise—not through violence, terrorism, or the killing of innocents—can you break out of a colonial prison.

Mickey, *mi pana*: all Latinos owe you for championing them so intelligently. *Mil gracias, compatriota.*

Jose Torres
2003

AFTER THIRTY YEARS

RAGE. IT TORE AT THE MUSCLES in my shoulders like fire. My limbs tensed and my throat dried out. My eyes struggled to focus. My whole body was consumed with anger so intense, it quickly turned to a burning desire for vengeance. What was I capable of? One thing was certain—I could no longer be passive. I would have to get involved. This fury had not visited me in years, but I remembered it well and knew what it meant: I would have to fight again.

It was April 21, 1999. I don't remember what New York City newspaper I was reading when I saw the short article about a civilian guard who had been killed by a bomb in Vieques, the island off the northeast coast of Puerto Rico. According to the newspaper, something had gone wrong during a United States

Navy target practice, and two 500-pound bombs exploded near the observation post, wounding several people and killing civilian David Sanes-Rodriguez. The incident took place on April 19, at around six o'clock, but it was not until hours later that the people in the nearby town learned about it. The story reached the mainland two days later.

The official report issued by the Navy called it an accident. Like many others, I was unconvinced.

When I returned home, my *compadre* Vicente Alba, telephoned me. He was also very upset about the events on Vieques and skeptical of the Navy's report. Alba, nicknamed "Panamá" after his country of origin, wanted to talk about how we should respond. The conversation was not short. There was too much to say, to think, to share. For us, and for a large and increasing number of Puerto Ricans, the death of David Sanes-Rodriguez was the latest in a long list of atrocities committed by the United States Government against our homeland.

After more than thirty years away from direct political action, I was about to rediscover my true vocation as an activist for social justice and for the independence of Puerto Rico. I wanted to hit the streets again. The death—or, more accurately, the killing— of David Sanes-Rodriguez at the hands of the U.S. Navy, was the spark plug that reignited my "activist" engine. His slaughter could not go unnoticed.

Panamá and I talked for hours that day, recalling similar previous tragedies. There was the Ponce Massacre in 1937 and the death of Don Pedro Albizu Campos in 1965. Don Pedro, who died after a long illness, was basically systematically killed by the long jail terms he had been forced to endure that severely damaged his health. He died for the "crime" of seeking for our Puerto Rican nation the same thing George Washington wanted for the American colonies: independence.

Don Pedro was born in Ponce, on the southern coast of Puerto Rico, in 1891. He was a brilliant student from the beginning; and even though his family was from the lower middle class, he was able to earn his degree from Harvard Law School. After serving as an officer in the then–racially segregated United States Army during World War One, Don Pedro turned to politics and became president of the Nationalist Party in Puerto Rico. In that position he influenced the independence movement, bringing in ideas he had learned from the nationalist revolutionary struggle in Ireland. He understood the Northern Irish battle for freedom from the colonial claws of Great Britain, and supported the Irish Republican Army's Sinn Fein Party ("Ourselves Alone"), a radical group of freedom fighters. In them, Don Pedro found inspiration as well as insight into successful political resistance tactics.

His intelligence and vision, as well as his stoic commitment to Puerto Rico's independence, attracted many followers, and the fact that he was nonwhite made him popular, particularly among the working class and the sugarcane workers who saw him as uncorrupted by the predominantly Caucasian elite. He quickly became a champion of the workingman and was called to represent the sugarcane workers during a general strike in 1934, one of the largest working-class demonstrations ever seen in Puerto Rico.

From then on, Don Pedro fell victim to the repressive forces of the United States' colonial government. A series of bloody encounters between security forces and the Nationalists followed. In 1937, Don Pedro was charged with conspiring to overthrow by force the U.S. Government in Puerto Rico. He was sent to federal prison in Atlanta, with many other Nationalist Party leaders; thus began his ordeal as an inmate for most of the rest of his life. He returned to Puerto Rico in 1947—but in 1950, when members of the Nationalist Party attacked the governor's mansion in Puerto Rico and Blair House in Washington, D.C., simultaneously, Don Pedro was charged with inciting murder and again imprisoned. He was pardoned in 1953 due to his failing health, but the pardon was revoked the following year when he was implicated in the armed attack on the United States House of Representatives on March 1, 1954. Sentenced to life in prison, Don Pedro's health deteriorated quickly, and he suffered a stroke in 1956. Death was imminent in 1964, and his sentence was commuted. When his body was examined after his death, it showed signs of torture by radiation, confirming Don Pedro's constant assertion that the U.S. was experimenting with radiation in prisons throughout the country.

Shortly after Don Pedro was first sent to federal prison in 1937, the Colonial Police—under the control of Governor Blanton Winship, a retired U.S. Army general who had been appointed governor of Puerto Rico by President Franklin Delano Roosevelt—opened fire on participants of a Nationalist Party rally in Ponce. The brutal police action, resulting in more than one hundred civilians wounded, twenty-one dead, including two policemen, and more than two hundred arrests, is remembered as "the Ponce Massacre" in Puerto Rican history books. According to the U.S. Government, it never happened. Washington has never issued a formal apology to the people of Puerto Rico.

For some, these events are history—that is, they belong only to the past, to the realm of memory. As history, they may inspire resentment, but not much more. However, for me and for many others, these past crimes are very much a part of the present. The truth of this became clear as I read about David Sanes-Rodriguez, only the most recent in a long line of victims.

Therefore, this book is not about resentment or revenge, but about setting the historical record straight.

In November 1999, Panamá telephoned me again. He recalled our previous conversation and told me that there was going to be a meeting of organizations and individuals willing to do something concrete to protest the U.S. Navy's presence in Vieques. In the wake of Sanes-Rodriguez's death, the decades-long struggle of the people of Vieques to end the U.S. Navy's use of the island for live-ammunition maneuvers had reached a new, higher pitch. For the first time, all political parties, churches, civic groups, and other community-based organizations spoke with a single voice: "Stop the Bombing Now! U.S. Navy Out of Vieques!" For the first time it seemed that six million Puerto Ricans (four million living on the main islands, and two million abroad) could present a solid and united resistance against the Navy.

Success seemed possible, and, reinvigorated, I agreed to accompany Panamá to this meeting, held at the Local Union 1199 headquarters in midtown Manhattan.

That labor union lives up to the motto—"Stronger Together"—inscribed in the lobby of its headquarters. It was the preferred union of Dr. Martin Luther King, Jr. It has always been sympathetic to social issues. Many of the health-care workers of the city's hospital system belong to it, as well as other service employees. More than a hundred of the victims of the September 11, 2001, tragedy were members of 1199. African-Americans, Puerto Ricans, and other Latinos comprise the majority of the membership.

Union president Dennis Rivera is a Puerto Rican who has distinguished himself by becoming a very powerful political strategist. Rivera's personal commitment in support of Vieques has been well documented since 1980, when he was still a young long-haired and bearded union activist and an advocate for Puerto Rican independence. Dennis was able to persuade environmental lawyer Robert Kennedy Jr. and Edward James Olmos to join in the struggle over Vieques, and the three of them endured a one-month jail term in federal prison in Puerto Rico for participating in a demonstration of civil disobedience during U.S. Navy maneuvers.

The night of that November 1999 meeting was chilly. Almost everyone there was either Puerto Rican or had some strong relationship with the Puerto Rican community in New York. It should have been a joyful occasion for me, but it wasn't. Much to my disappointment, present were the same old radicals of thirty years ago, with the same old gusto for endless theoretical discussions and emotional speeches, but who never gather enough willpower and determination to actually *do* something. Certainly, their thorough assessment of the Vieques problem was not without value. But we knew the history. We needed a plan of action, not endless rhetoric.

After nearly one hour of listening to The Left, I attracted Panamá's attention with a discreet signal, and we quietly moved to the back of the ample room. I don't have much tolerance for what I was listening to. It's as bad as right-wing bullshit.

"This is too frustrating for me," I complained to my *compadre*. I told him the moment was right to create a media event through direct political action. My old comrade-in-arms had always been open to finding creative ways to make a point. What we needed to do was not that complex: engage in a civil disobedience, get arrested, and hit the news media. No need to talk much about this simple, yet highly effective type of 1–2–3 action.

By the end of the meeting, the group had reached the only obvious conclusion—to continue the discussion at another meeting. Panamá and I decided to do the same, but our meeting the next day had a very different agenda. As soon as the meeting started, we began compiling a list of names of people we thought would be willing to work with us on a direct action. Once we had come up with twenty names, we decided to think of a name for the group. Without question it would be called a "brigade." It seemed appropriate for the type of attack we were preparing, and it is historically resonant of earlier revolutionary groups, like the Venceremos Brigade, which for over three decades has brought together people from several nations in a mission to help Cuba. The members of the Venceremos Brigade travel to Cuba, dwell there, and work along with the Cubans, thus giving a practical meaning to the word "solidarity."

The use of the term "brigade" served another useful purpose. Neither Panamá nor myself is a pacifist, and the military designation "brigade" would make that clear. We wanted peace for Vieques, but we weren't necessarily going to obtain it through peaceful means. I respect true pacifists, but they are few, and I've found the ranks of "pacifists" teeming with far too many hypocrites for my liking. Rather than Mahatma Gandhi, my role models are people who have risked their lives and possessions in their quest for freedom: Simón Bolívar, Che Guevara, Ho Chi Minh, Don Pedro.

Taking all of this into consideration, we finally christened ourselves La Brigada David Sanes-Rodriguez—the David Sanes-Rodriguez Brigade—in order to honor Sanes' memory and to place him in a historical context. Our actions would be conducted in the name of a Puerto Rican killed by U.S. bombs on his own patio. This way it wouldn't be an anonymous struggle for a civil cause. No—we considered that since the whole idea was to educate the American public on the issue, portraying the fate of a specific human being would help people realize the real-life consequences of the military abuse of Vieques, Puerto Rico, with more than nine thousand souls living there.

A date for the action was also selected. The offensive was to begin December 7, 1999—the anniversary of the Japanese attack

on Pearl Harbor in 1941. The date was not selected out of dis-
respect for the many heroes in the struggle against fascism; too
many people, including soldiers in the Puerto Rican Sixty-fifth
Infantry Regiment, died fighting to end World War Two. But
the cold and impersonal way David Sanes-Rodriguez's killing in
Vieques was originally ignored by the Navy's top brass suggested
that, to them, the Puerto Rican man was less than human. His
slaughter represented a "Day of Infamy" for us. Our purpose on
that day was to let America know that, "You didn't like getting
bombed, neither do we—'U.S. Navy out of Vieques.' " Someone
had to remind the United States and the world that the struggle
against such abuses was far from over in Puerto Rico. Someone
had to tell the American public that while many sacrifices by our
people were justifiably required during World War Two, the
continuation of the live-ammunition naval maneuvers on a pop-
ulated island, more than fifty years after the end of the war, is
criminal.

After our short meeting, I went back home and immediately
began calling the twenty names on our list. We were on the
move.

Recruiting the members of the brigade was not difficult. Many
people were more than ready to be arrested. Still, of the twenty
names Panamá and I gathered, ten came forward: Luis Garden
Acosta, Jose "Chegüí" Torres, Gladys Peña, Reverend Luis Barrios, Juan Figueroa, Samuel Sánchez, Rosa Cruz, Lissette Nieves,
William Gerena, and me. Panamá would not get arrested and he
would handle the press. We knew from experience that the number of participants in an action mattered less than their level of
commitment. A small, dedicated group could be just as effective,

even more so, than a large army. After all, you don't need many matches to start a fire.

Early in the morning on December 7, 1999, the eleven-member brigade assembled in front of the New York City Public Library on Fifth Avenue. As I approached the building, it was clear to me that police intelligence agents were present in the area. After thirty years of activism you can smell them anywhere. I wasn't surprised. We'd leaked information of the protest to the police—with one critical red herring. The police thought our target was the USS *Intrepid*, the World War Two aircraft carrier anchored in the Hudson River, now a museum. It certainly would be a great target for a demonstration, but we had our sights set elsewhere. Until that morning, only Panamá and I knew where we were really headed. The others in La Brigada David Sanes-Rodriguez trusted us enough to put themselves in our hands until the very last moment, and had agreed in advance to be arrested for civil disobedience. After everyone arrived, we began marching west on 42nd Street toward the Hudson River, but then we crossed north, and turned east toward the United Nations building, our real target.

The move, unexpected by the police, gave us the time we needed to chain ourselves to the gate in front of the employee entrance to the building. I had arranged for two former Young Lords, Juan González and Pablo Guzmán, to meet us there. Both are now distinguished journalists. Juan is an award-winning columnist for the *New York Daily News*, and Pablo is a reporter for CBS-TV. Joining them was José Rosario, the award-winning photographer for *El Diario/la prensa*, one of the largest Spanish-language newspapers in the country. The presence of both print and broadcast press was crucial. By the time the NYPD recovered from their surprise—thinking about it still makes me laugh—and figured out where we were, we were already positioned in an area where it was unclear who would have the legal authority to make arrests: the U.N. guards or the New York City Police.

Now we were blocking one of the entrances to the U.N. While the two groups of security officers conferred on the issue of jurisdiction, Rubén Blades, the Panamanian-born singer, actor, and international human-rights advocate, agreed to read a statement to the press expressing solidarity with the grievances of the Puerto Rican people regarding Vieques. Reverend Luis Barrios of San Romero de las Americas Church read from the Bible and presided over prayers for our brothers and sisters in Vieques. Both elements—Latin American solidarity and the Church's benediction—are very important for Puerto Ricans. Our communities remain isolated from mainstream America and very little is really known about Puerto Rico. What is Puerto Rico? Where is it? Who cares?

According to the U.S. Supreme Court, Puerto Rico belongs to, but is not part of, the United States. If that judicial point of view is taken seriously, then Puerto Rico is a belonging, a possession. Can one nation possess another? Can you imagine someone saying that the United States belongs to, but is not part of, another nation?

Puerto Rico is a Latin American/Caribbean nation with a history longer than that of the independent United States. Its people form a very distinct culture, with its own sense of common origin and destiny. Although several attempts were made to liberate Puerto Ricans from Spanish rule, Puerto Rico remained a colony of His Majesty the King of Spain until the Spanish-American War of 1898. Since then, Puerto Rico has, under one official name or another, essentially been under the thumb of the United States. Under its current status as a commonwealth, Puerto Ricans have all of the rights and obligations of United

States citizens, including military service, but do not pay federal taxes and do not participate in national elections. So, Puerto Ricans on the island do not vote for the President of the United States, but young Puerto Ricans are obligated to kill or die in U.S. military conflicts around the world. Puerto Ricans finally elected their own governor in 1952. Some are quite happy with the perceived political and economic benefits of commonwealth status. Others would like to erase the ambiguity by making Puerto Rico the fifty-first state. For me, neither of these possibilities addresses the heart of the matter: that Puerto Rico has been passed like a child's toy from colonial hand to colonial hand without the people's consent. Independence, an inalienable human right, is the only politically, economically and socially just answer. Without autonomy, Puerto Rico will remain a dependent colony of the United States, no matter what new names the government in Washington may dream up to call it. The U.S. Government will never admit this. It just doesn't sound democratic. And it isn't. Thus Puerto Rico remains at the crossroads in the poorly defined border between the Protestant Anglo-Saxon America to the north, and Catholic Latin America to the south.

The experience is harsher for the Puerto Ricans living or born away from the island. For instance, I was born in New York, but had to learn about Puerto Rico outside the classroom. For me, as well as for millions of Puerto Ricans in the United States, solidarity and faith are important tools in our "survival kits," the type of resource you never leave your house without.

The mixture of solidarity and religion in our demonstration in front of the U.N. building was not intended to manipulate the media, but was truly an effort to express ourselves, to affirm who we are. However, we did manipulate the *circumstances* in order to prevent the arrests until we had time to conduct our ceremony. Having accomplished that, we had no problem being arrested. Panamá cut the plastic handcuffs we were using to chain ourselves to the entrance; that way we avoided prosecution for obstructing justice. When everything was ready, the arrests began. At that moment I thought: *We have just won!*

We were a small group of people staging a peaceful protest against the use of our motherland as a bombing target, and we were being arrested. There was no physical threat to anyone's safety to warrant our being placed into custody. But there is no such thing as a minor threat when someone fails to obey the established order. We were breaking the law, so they had to arrest us. But they successfully helped us get our grievances aired, and printed in the headlines.

First to be arrested was former 1956 Olympic light-middleweight champion, Jose "Chegüí" Torres. The second was me. I felt nothing. The moment for emotions and concerns had been the night before. Of my four children, two live on the West Coast, and two are in New York. I took the ones in New York with me to Willie's Steak House in the Bronx for dinner. It was a pleasant evening. Then I told them there would be an action that would take place the day after, and that there was a strong possibility I would be arrested. They reacted with concern. The fact that they know about my political commitment did not prevent them from worrying about what would happen if something went wrong. Although everything had been carefully planned to force the police to execute arrests rather symbolically, it was going to be the first civil-disobedience operation related to Vieques ever to take place in the U.S. We made it historic—not for us, but for David Sanes-Rodriguez and Vieques.

Nothing had gone wrong so far. Two police officers faced me. I noticed from their badges that they had Spanish surnames. But, there was no hint of "*I am with you*" in their eyes, at least not until later when we got to the precinct. One of them read me my Miranda rights while the other stood motionless, looking passively at my face. Then the first one asked if I wanted to be arrested. I answered, "Yes," and the other policeman went behind me, took both my forearms and crossed them behind my lower back. I remained composed and tried to look as phlegmatic as they did. There was not a single trace of bad feelings in me. During those seconds when the TV cameras were rolling, we all felt great. The policeman behind my back secured my forearms with plastic handcuffs then grabbed one of my arms.

I saw from the corner of my eye two other policemen begin the same ceremony with art curator Gladys Peña, who was next to me. While the same routine began with her, I was taken to the paddy wagon where Chegüí was already seated. With my arms immobilized by the handcuffs, I was unable to climb into the police wagon and the policeman had to help me up. In a matter of minutes we were all in the vehicle, seated in two lines on the benches facing each other. The doors were closed and we started the ride toward the Seventeenth Precinct.

If you walked from the U.N. building to the Seventeenth Precinct, it would take less than ten minutes to get there. But the police van took a long time—more than thirty minutes—to reach our destination, due to the never-ending traffic jams of midtown Manhattan.

We were in a joyful mood, making fun of everything. It was the emotional release that comes with winning . . . with beating The State. Someone said that the short trip could take more than a day, and everybody laughed with gusto. We kept chanting slogans—*"Si la marina no se va, en Vieques morirán"* ("If the marines don't leave, in Vieques they will die")—and singing patriotic songs like, *"Que bonita bandera es la bandera puertorriqueña"* ("What a beautiful flag is the Puerto Rican flag") all the way.

Inside the Seventeenth Precinct it was a more serious affair, where intelligence officers conducted the interrogations. No more "good cop/bad cop" like when I in was visited by the FBI the 1960s. Now they send in two "good" cops. I thought their civility may have had something to do with the sensitive and potentially explosive nature of the sociopolitical situation. The Vieques issue is an emotional one for Latinos in general and Puerto Ricans in particular. The police claimed to have an understanding of Puerto Rico's plight, but said they needed to know how the operation was prepared and whether or not we were planning another demonstration.

In their interrogation of me, the intelligence officers were trying to get what they thought could help them defeat further attempts by the Puerto Rican people to raise national and international support for Vieques. They got only what they have been getting from me for many years: nothing. However, a part of me felt it was time they received an answer of some kind—although not necessarily the one they had been waiting for.

They wanted to know the origins of our defiant action. They asked for a history lesson. With Juan Figeroa, co-defendant and attorney, at my side I looked them in the eye and began "Puerto Rican History of Vieques 101."

Back in the late 1930s, President Franklin Delano Roosevelt visited Vieques and eastern Puerto Rico to conduct an inspection of naval maneuvers. Roosevelt also gave his final approval for the Navy's request to establish a large base in the area. Robert Rabin, director of Vieques' historical archives, has recently provided a summary that points out how the land of Vieques was seized by the Navy. His summary describes the numerous abuses against the population and how, after the end of World War Two, Puerto

Rico's request for a withdrawal of the U.S. fleet in order to address the economic problems of Vieques was ignored by federal
authorities. Rabin also mentioned the plans made by the U.S.
Navy under President John F. Kennedy to evict all the people
from Vieques in order to have the whole island available as a
target for fighting planes and ships. The list of the Navy's abuses
against Vieques is long. Sanes-Rodriguez's death served only as
a catalyst to spread a struggle that had been developing for decades. Among many other tragedies was the killing of Angel
Rodríguez Cristóbal in the Tallahassee, Florida, federal prison
after being arrested and charged with trespassing during a civil-
disobedience action against the Navy in 1979.

The Vieques issue has awakened the history of the unsolved
border struggle between Latin America and Anglo America. The
book *Foxardo 1824 and the Ritual Bombing of Vieques*, by journalist
Jesús Dávila in 2002, traces the background of the case to the
early nineteenth century. What the Navy may have done with
its stubborn attitude is to revive admiration for Simón Bolívar
and other heroes of liberty from Venezuela, Columbia, Panama,
Mexico, Cuba, and other Caribbean nations. Not only are health,
environmental destruction, and human-rights issues at stake, but
also native Caribbean identity, the perpetual lack of respect of
the United States for Latin America, and the threats to hemi-
spheric security and stability created by conducting military maneuvers in Vieques.

To understand the strategic importance of Vieques, it must
be seen within the context of its geographical position in the
West Indies. That string of small islands, in the eastern Caribbean, comprises a barrier that separates the Latin American continent from the Atlantic westbound routes. Control of these
islands can give any empire the power to curtail or encourage
trade between Latin America, the United States, Europe, and

the Caribbean island nations. In the early nineteenth century, almost all of Latin America won its independence; the United States gave its endorsement as long as the islands of the Lesser and Greater Antilles were kept under strict colonial control. France, England, Holland, and even Spain retained their respective Antillean possessions. By the end of that century, even the United States began acquiring its own colonies in the area, with Puerto Rico in 1898 and the Virgin Islands in 1917. In the second half of the twentieth century, Caribbean islands like Grenada, Jamaica, and Barbados became increasingly interested in independence, and several of the island nations became autonomous.

If you look at this development with democratic values in mind, it can be understood as a triumph of democracy and freedom. But one of the saddest lessons the Latin American nations have learned from America is that while the United States highly regards democracy as an inalienable right for its citizens, it too often opposes democracy when the torch of liberty is raised south of the border. "Imperialism" describes America's involvement with Latin America.

Between 1980 and 1986, the U.S. military budget assigned to the eastern Caribbean under the euphemism of "aid" skyrocketed from $200,000 to $20 million. What was the aim? To furnish a string of training and operational bases from which to strengthen naval control of the area. Who gave that power to the United States? Nobody. The last years of the Cold War were particularly harsh for the eastern Caribbean. The region had to endure hardships such as the invasion of Grenada in 1983 because the Reagan administration felt that country's building an airport with Cuban and Soviet aid posed a communist threat to the United States.

Vieques played a pivotal role in the military buildup. Besides containing a firing range, the island is at the center of two large oceanic areas for naval warfare—one in the Atlantic and the other in the Caribbean Sea. The second one, dubbed "Bravo," reaches from south of Vieques to almost the northern coast of Venezuela, and along all the shores of the Lesser Antilles. Who are the enemies here? From what evil advance is that naval "Maginot Line" protecting us? Up until the late 1980s we were told that it protected us from the communists. The Soviet Union is gone. And to say that such a mammoth naval barrier would protect the U.S. mainland from drug trafficking amounts to confessing sheer ignorance on the subject of drug smuggling. What other issue can be raised as an excuse? The reality is that the only threat to freedom and democracy is that imposed by U.S. foreign policy in the area.

The case becomes clearer when the Vieques issue is seen from a historical perspective. Dávila states that there is no real naval use for the Vieques facility. There is no actual training going on there, although it is the site of many maneuvers and bombings, which serve the purpose of a show of force. From the U.S. Navy's standpoint, Vieques is a symbol of naval pride and imperial dreams. For Latin America, Vieques is full of meaning; therefore it is a Latin American issue, as well as an international hot spot regarding issues of aggression and economic dominance.

What other building, then, would be a more appropriate site for our demonstration than the U.N.? As I concluded my lesson I told them that they were helpless in the struggle for justice in Vieques. There will undoubtedly be more actions, and "you will not know, when or where—that is for us to decide."

I told the police I had nothing else to say and asked to be returned to the holding pen. From December 7, 1999, to the end of 2002, there were civil disobedience actions in San Francisco,

Connecticut, New Jersey, and Washington, D.C. On May 5, 2000, Representative Jose Serrano was arrested in front of the White House, and seventy-five protesters were arrested in September 2000 in the Capital. There were twelve actions in New York City, including Yankee Stadium (seven arrested), and at the Statue of Liberty (eleven arrested), resulting in over 270 arrests in the U.S.

Back in the cell, the party continued. We were making jokes and laughing, with the Reverend Barrios revealing his talent for stand-up comedy. Ministers like Barrios, who combine their faith with firm commitment to the people and such a fine sense of humor, leave us no doubt that we are spiritually in exceptional hands.

Meanwhile, Chegüí was a sensation. A man who was in the cell with us surprised everybody by asking the guard to lend him a pen in order to get his autograph. The policeman not only acquiesced, but also asked our champ for an autograph for himself.

At one moment I looked toward Luis Garden Acosta, who had dropped out of Harvard to head the Boston branch of the Young Lords, and said to him: "Luis, it was in 1969 that the Young Lords was founded, so this is like a thirtieth-anniversary celebration."

"I didn't realize it's been thirty years," Luis said with his broad smile.

We had found yet another way to enjoy this occasion. But then it hit me: After three decades I was now under arrest for the same ideals I had fought for back then. How had I arrived at the very same place I had started? Time stopped. I moved to the back of the cell, feeling incredibly alone. I sat down on the bench and ceased to pay attention to the increasingly distant anecdotes and cheerful conversations. I was in jail and had some time to reflect. A desire to close my eyes engulfed me. I needed to find something, understand something—my story, my movie, my truth.

Thirty years had passed since the founding of the Young Lords. Could it be so? Were we meant to be the Young Lords even before the whole idea was conceived by us? Looking into my own personal life, it became clear this had been a long journey. The voices of my co-conspirators had grown faint, I could barely hear their laughter.

My thoughts drifted back to my beginnings . . .

BEGINNINGS

FOR ALL ITS INFLUENCE on people's lives, history often seems more like a silent cloud than a guiding hand. No matter how subtle or silent, our history has a profound influence on our present and our future. If we search carefully enough, its path can be traced through the deeds and hopes of our ancestors to the very source and foundation of ourselves. You either claim your history or you lose authority over your future. The mist I must row into withers away slowly, letting me only glimpse the colors and outlines of events. It's an experience that may be common to all human beings, but for people like my family, known to the world as Latino, Hispano, and/or Hispanic-American—or, more specifically, Puerto Rican, Cuban, or Nuyorican—our history, which always begins somewhere other than New York City, is very important.

Even for those of us born in the United States, we can't escape the fact that we are sons and daughters of migrants who have come from places far beyond these shores. For my *Boricua* (Puerto Rican) side, there is a common history as well as a unique family chronicle that has shaped each and every one of us. I guess that's why Puerto Ricans love to tell family stories. Embodied in all of our accounts is the whole history of our dreams, hopes, and struggles—from early encounters with the Spanish conquistadores and the Taíno Indians, through the history of slavery to the present diaspora created by our commonwealth status. Through it all, we weave the threads of legend, gallantry, and conquest, of romance, sacrifice, defeats, and sometimes hard-earned victories.

My story belongs within the family that represents a third of the Puerto Rican population: those who have left the island. A combination of economic hardships and United States governmental policies that encouraged emigration forms the base of my story. It's the history of United States expansionism in the Caribbean, the story of my father, and his mother and father, ill-treated by colonization, the story of millions of Puerto Ricans now spread throughout every state of the Union.

The land, named Puerto Rico by Spanish explorer Juan Ponce de León, was originally inhabited by the Taíno Indians, an Arawak people. They had migrated north into the Caribbean from the Orinoco River delta in Venezuela in *"pirágüas,"* a type of canoe. The Taíno called the region "Boriquén" (loosely translated: "the Land of the High Lord," or "valiant land"). There is a high mountain almost always crowned by haze that the Taínos called the House of Yukiyú the Supreme God. Near the main island, the Taínos also inhabited a smattering of smaller ones called *cayes*, named Mona, Culebra, and Vieques.

Christopher Columbus, or Cristóbal Colón, first sighted this land in 1493, during his second expedition to the region. He named the island San Juan Bautista, but didn't stay long enough to establish a settlement. De León began the actual conquest of the island in 1508. It wasn't long before the original inhabitants and their thriving culture were decimated by disease, hardship, and Spanish massacres. Some were able to escape into the mountains (cimarrones) where they found refuge and laid the foundation for a new people, a new nation. The full story of the Taínos who survived is unknown. What is known, though, is that once the Taínos had seemingly vanished, the Spanish desperately needed a new labor force to work their plantations and gold mines. They were forced to import slave labor from Africa, forever changing the ethnic makeup of the island. As San Juan, the island's capital, became a leading outpost of the Empire, and home to well-provisioned Spanish galleons, Puerto Rico became a target for buccaneers and other cutthroats. Spanish discipline was harsh during this period, and so scores of Spanish peasants, slaves, and other fugitives sought refuge in the mountains, where they started to intermarry with the surviving Taínos. Those first natives renamed the mountain forests as El Yunque. There, in the Taíno environs, was birthed a new breed of human beings: the Puerto Rican Jíbaro. And while the Jíbaros began to establish their own way of life in the mountains, as far away from the Spanish Crown as they could get, life in the colonial enclaves became unbearable. Hunger and disease made living conditions miserable, and Spanish ire increased due to the diminishing natural resources of the island, particularly the lack of gold. Many fled to Peru, enticed by rumors of gold.

Yet, by the early nineteenth century, Puerto Rico was forging a national identity and a unified voice. As many inhabitants left the island to escape tyranny, others organized revolutionary groups with the hope of overthrowing the government. Revolutionaries on the islands collaborated with others in New York, Paris, and London. Puerto Ricans, Cubans, and Dominicans joined forces to fight Spain's oppressive regime. These voices got stronger during the second half of the nineteenth century. In 1868, for example, Dr. Ramón Emeterio Betances organized a large rebellion of Puerto Rican nationalists known as "El Grito de Lares," and proclaimed Puerto Rico's independence as well as the abolition of slavery. Betances bought slaves at the marketplace and then set them free right before Spanish eyes. Because of his work, slavery was finally officially abolished in 1873, and the press was allowed to discuss political and economic conditions on the island—even openly slur members of the Cortes. Just as Cubans consider Jose Marti to be the father of their country, Puerto Ricans look on Betances as el Padre de la Patria. In 1897, largely through the work of Don Luis Muñoz Rivera, Puerto Rico was able to gain a form of autonomy from Spain. The arrangement lasted a very short time, however. After the sinking of the USS *Maine*, the United States began the Spanish-American War, and U.S. troops landed on the island and occupied it in July of 1898 with little difficulty. The 'Treaty of Paris,' which ended the war five months later in December, ceded Puerto Rico, Guam, Cuba, and the Philippines to the United States, and Spanish domination of the region became history.

With the exception of Aguila Blanca—"White Eagle," who, with a band of guerrillas fought the United States troops now occupying the island—and Betances, who stated shortly before his death that he would not accept one form of colonialism for another—many welcomed the transition of power. For many believed that Puerto Rico would be given more respect and autonomy from a democratic nation like the United States. This belief, however, was soon shattered. The Foraker Act, passed in 1900, gave Puerto Ricans limited self-rule. The governor and upper legislative chamber were to be appointed by the United States president. The Jones Act of 1917 eased matters only slightly by bestowing United States citizenship upon Puerto Ricans, and providing for the election of both legislative houses in Puerto Rico. But the governor and other key officials still would be appointed by the president. During World War One, United States holdings on the island increased and sugarcane became the dominant crop. Life in Puerto Rico became unbearable as the population spiked, and the sugar market plummeted in the 1930s as a result of the The Great Depression in the States.

My paternal grandparents worked on the sugar plantations under brutal working and living conditions during the early part of the century. Like thousands of others, they eventually decided to try their luck in San Juan. My grandfather settled in a blue-collar neighborhood in the capital, close to the docks, where he hoped to find work. These neighborhoods were not shantytowns, but working-class areas also known as *barrios obreros*, or workers' wards. Though poor, people here lived better than their counterparts in the *campos*. The city had grown in recent years, its boundaries spreading into the surrounding farmland. One of the newly incorporated areas was Santurce, a barrio with a mosaic of neighborhoods made up of diverse social classes. In one of the areas where blue-collar workers lived, not far from San Agustín y Calle Ocho, my grandfather, Juan Meléndez, had established his family and business. This is where my story begins.

Life was simple: You worked hard and hoped for the best. *Mi abuelito* had a shoe-repair shop named *Zapatería el Combate* and had been among the first on the entire island to modernize his small business by purchasing an electric repair machine. Such a promising beginning turned out to be a heartbreaking prologue; Juan Meléndez died suddenly at the young age of thirty-three. Many in the family still believe his death was caused by the toxic fumes of his trade. As a result, my grandmother Micaela was left with six children to support on her meager salary as a grade-school custodian. This tragedy marked the beginning of my father Miguel's wandering.

It was common in Puerto Rico under such circumstances to send young daughters to live with relatives, and young sons to all-boy orphanages. Miguel, the youngest boy, at age five, was placed in one such orphanage. It is difficult to know for certain, but at eighty-nine he remembers being sent to the one in Santurce, a two-story building with masonry walls, near the waterfront. It still stands to this day. Though now fully part of the historic city, back then it would have looked extremely far from home for any young boy.

Miguel spent two years in the orphanage until his homesickness became so unbearable that he ran away. At age seven, he was back in the circle of his mother's warmth, but also faced the harsh realities of life in Santurce. During his childhood, Miguel worked at odd jobs throughout the barrio to help support his family. It was difficult to work and get an education at the same time. Many young people simply dropped out to work full-time. Miguel persevered, and his graduation at eighteen from Jose Celso Barbosa Junior High School was one of the happiest moments of his life, and the accomplishment he was always most proud of. Even more satisfying was that this was the same educational institution that had once employed his mother as a cleaning lady.

Even now, years later, he still reminds me that an eighth-grade diploma from "La Barbosa," is the equivalent of a high-school diploma anywhere in America. Secondary education was not common in Puerto Rico in those years, and often, outstand-ing eighth-grade graduates were hired to teach elementary school. After graduation, Miguel continued to do many menial jobs. In one lucky break, he was able to get a well-paying job in one of the development projects sponsored by the Puerto Rico Reconstruction Act (PRRA) program, part of Franklin Delano Roosevelt's New Deal policy. By age twenty, however, Miguel was dissatisfied with such irregular work. He decided to go to the local offices of the Ford Motor Company in San Juan and managed to get a job as a porter for 15 cents an hour—a fortune, considering that most peasants earned less than 25 cents a day washing floors and automobiles.

The early 1930s were especially tough times in Puerto Rico. The economic crisis was not the only problem and certainly not the worst one. A sense of betrayal and repression permeated the air. The U.S. Government continued to exercise complete con-trol over the island, through what many felt was a corrupt po-litical system. As the conservative, pro-America Party won election after election in Puerto Rico, many people became in-creasingly exasperated. Nationalists were prevented from organ-izing a resistance effort by a militarized police force that loved to answer words with bullets.

My father left San Juan in 1936, long before the sweeping economic and social reforms of "Operation Bootstrap" swept the island. Designed to industrialize and urbanize the island, Oper-ation Bootstrap became an Americanizing force on the Puerto Rican people, encouraging American business on the island while promoting migration to the mainland. Although the economy started to pick up, the price was steep. Local culture, even the local language, was threatened. English-language teachers, for example, were imported to all public schools on the island in order to force children to speak English. While the rest of my father's family struggled through these traumatic times, he decided it was time to leave.

What made him decide to go? I often wonder just what it was that compelled him to squeeze on board a ship docked in San Juan, bound for the north, at the young age of twenty-two, leaving behind everything and everyone he'd ever known. He spent the next thirty-three years as a merchant marine, eventually working his way up to oilman. Merchant ships prior to World War Two were not like those of today. The cargo was not loaded in containers, but in boxes, crocks, and barrels. Although they were steam-powered, commercial cargo ships were more like nineteenth-century sailing ships, with large crews, and less and smaller tonnage. Sometimes they even carried a couple of passengers.

In one of those merchant ships my father sailed to Boston, a major destination for Puerto Rican exports in the first half of the twentieth century. It was not that New York meant little for Puerto Rico's foreign trade, but most of the colonial corporations engaged in trade were based in Boston. When Puerto Rico was incorporated into the federal judicial system of the United States, instead of assigning the Federal District Court of Puerto Rico to New York—which would be more logical today—it became (and still is) part of Boston's First Circuit Court of Appeals.

Meanwhile New York City had become the main attraction for Puerto Rican migrant workers. Most began to establish a Puerto Rican community on the south side of the Williamsburg section in Brooklyn, soon becoming known as "Los Sures." To the southwest, on Columbia Street, was the Brooklyn pier where the SS *Marine Tiger* usually docked, the most famous vessel among Puerto Rican workers willing to come to America to earn a better living. So many of my people traveled from Puerto Rico to Brooklyn on the *Marine Tiger,* that the newly arrived were nicknamed "Marine Tigers." Other steamships, like the *Coamo* (named after a small southern town in Puerto Rico), were known as passenger ships, but none had the same aura of modern human-cargo traffic between Puerto Rico and the United States as the *Marine Tiger* did.

Ironically, Miguel didn't come over in the *Marine Tiger*, nor did he establish his home in Brooklyn. He came from Boston by bus in 1936 and went straight to Spanish Harlem, which stretched from 96th to 125th Street between First Avenue and Madison, and was soon to become the most important Puerto Rican haven in New York. The neighborhood was promptly dubbed "El Barrio."

The Puerto Rican presence in New York goes back to the 1830s, when the young heirs of the island's plantations and Puerto Rican merchants came to the bustling metropolis, mostly as students or trade envoys. In the 1890s, New York became a refuge for Caribbean revolutionaries, Puerto Ricans among them. While the first wave was more related to trade, the second one had the imprint of high culture as well as wealth. One early arrival was Dr. Jose Julio Henna, who lived in a mansion on Fifth Avenue, near the current location of the main branch of the New York Public Library. He was one of the leading physicians of the French Hospital. Another pioneer was Arturo Schomburg, a Puerto Rican who devoted himself to the study of his African roots, and became a cornerstone of the Harlem Renaissance. At one point Schomburg joined Jose Marti, and his Cuban Revolutionary Party in New York; he is also revered as the founder of African and African-American studies in the United States and his name is honored with the Schomburg Center for Research in Black Culture in Harlem. With the United States invasion of Puerto Rico in 1898 during the Spanish-American War, Puerto Ricans' migration to New York City increased heavily. Immigration became more intense after 1917, when the Jones Act passed in Washington, D.C., giving Puerto Ricans United States citizenship—just in time to fight in World War One.

Miguel, called "Mike" by his non-Latino merchant marine friends, was not a historian. Neither was he a political exile or a revolutionary. He was a sailor who wanted to become part of New York City's diverse community. After all, this city had the largest and busiest port in the world, the perfect spot for a young man to look for an apartment, settle in, and get his share of romance. Not surprisingly, he got more than he bargained for.

From the beginning Miguel was considered a marginal success among the poor people of El Barrio. He was a dapper dresser, sporting a halfback's body with a ten-gallon Stetson hat, looking more like George Raft with a Rudolph Valentino mustache than a cargo-ship wiper. In addition, he was a card-carrying member of the National Maritime Union, one of those special men who were able to visit distant places and return with fabulous souvenirs like Spanish Maja soap, perfumes, European canaries, and Carlos I and Philipe II brandies. He made a decent salary and made a little extra money selling the products he picked up overseas on the streets of the barrio.

In those days, the streets belonged to the men. Miguel, young and with plenty of resources by El Barrio standards, would be expected to have a few bachelor adventures before settling down. Either by virtue or destiny, these were not in store for him. Soon after his arrival in New York, he fell in love with a beautiful sixteen-year-old girl he'd spotted from the street, at the window of a high apartment with her arms resting on the sill. As soon as she noticed the young man below staring at her, she vanished into the apartment. Her disappearing act was too late. My father was already mesmerized by her. Miguel stood every day on the sidewalk in front of the girl's building, waiting for her to appear at the window. As soon as she did, he would wave his arms to the sky and then down to the sidewalk, signaling her to come down. But every time, the girl would disappear as soon as she noticed the young man in the street. This went on for weeks. It seemed impossible.

Eventually Miguel would learn through the barrio grapevine that her name was Celia, and that she had been brought to New York by her mother Aurora, who'd made the trip from Tampa with her second husband and five of her twelve children in two days straight. They also had come to New York looking for better jobs.

Since the nineteenth century, Tampa has been home to one of the largest Cuban-American communities in the United States, due mostly to its close proximity to the island. The Latino influence on Tampa goes back much farther than that, to the earliest Europeans settlers who arrived on this continent in the sixteenth century. Discovered by the governor of Puerto Rico, Don Juan Ponce de León, Florida remained a Spanish dominion, with an interlude of British intervention, well into the nineteenth century, when the United States bought it after the bloody conquering expedition of General Andrew Jackson.

The influx of immigrants after the Cuban Revolution in 1959 often obscures the rich and diverse history of Cubans in Florida during the early part of the twentieth century. From its earliest days, Tampa was considered the Miami of Florida, the center of Cuban culture, attracting a rich and diverse community. The Great Depression hit the area especially hard and took its toll, and many families like Celia's tried to escape by moving to the industrial Northeast. Not everybody left, though. Aurora's eldest son, Ernesto, stayed in Ybor City, Florida, working as a baker and was the head of "El Círculo Cubano," a social club.

After enduring the hard trip—even though the car they were

driving was a Cadillac, it did nothing to alleviate the discomfort they all suffered—Aurora arrived with the kids and her husband, Juan Díaz, on a frozen October 3, 1936. Luckily, as soon as they arrived in El Barrio, they bumped into a Tampeña who immediately directed them to where Uncle Josie, who had made the trip up north a few months before, was sharing a small apartment with two other roommates. Josie was making $7 a week working at the American Women's Association Hotel and couldn't afford much. The tiny apartment didn't have an icebox, and 5 cents for a block of ice was too expensive, so Josie used a cardboard box placed outside a window to keep milk and other foods fresh. A coal stove heated the apartment. On winter mornings everyone would wake up with soot coating their faces from the burnt coal. With the idea that "where one eats, so can two," the family of seven stayed at Josie's place while Aurora searched for an apartment. It took two weeks to find a more comfortable place with a real furnace. Celia and her family were still living in that second apartment when Miguel first saw her.

Miguel joked with his friends that maybe the beautiful girl had no legs, and so couldn't come down to see him. In time, his lucky day arrived. When she visited the nearby bodega he finally managed to meet her. Even virtuous young ladies come down eventually. The trim, fair-skinned, five-foot-tall young woman stole my father's heart for the second time.

More resolved than ever to gain Celia's affections, Miguel finagled permission from her family to court her in the traditional fashion. For the next two years, he visited Celia in the living room of her apartment, chaperoned, of course, by the entire family. Love found its way. On October 19, 1940, two years after Celia's arrival in New York, and a month before his twenty-fifth birthday, the persistent Miguel became the proud groom of a beautiful Tampeña princess.

Then the real work of building a marriage—and a lasting love—began. My father, a sailor, was away for long periods of time, and my mother was responsible for every aspect of daily life. She was alone often, and worked hard to make ends meet and do the daily chores. The situation became more stressful when the United States entered World War Two. As a sailor my father was exempted from active duty since he was in the merchant marine, but not from the war effort. His cargo ship frequently crossed the Atlantic with enemy prisoners from France and Italy destined for the military concentration camps in Norfolk, Virginia, defying German U-boats along the way. When Celia found out she was pregnant with their first child, they moved to an apartment on 108th Street, only two blocks away from the Flower Fifth Avenue Hospital, and half a block from Central Park.

Moving near the hospital proved to be wise: my sister Helen was born prematurely and dangerously small, at seven months, on January 26, 1942. Three years later my mother miscarried twins. Even this tragedy didn't diminish the high regard my parents felt for the quality of caregiving at Flower Fifth Avenue Hospital. They were not a bit concerned when I was born on November 17, 1947, a seven-pound slightly tan-colored, healthy baby. Being the "Benjamin" of the family, the first boy, I was named Miguel Ernesto, paying honor to both my father and my mother's eldest brother. I spent my early days—until I was five—in El Barrio, with its open-all-night bodegas and the vibrant and always-noisy street. There you heard the ever-familiar expression *"¿Que pasa?"* all over the place, and saw small rubber balls flying through the air in wild games of stickball. At home my mother cooked only Cuban food and listened to Cuban music, as we ate black beans, white rice, and *ropa vieja* (shredded beef) in the dining room. When Daddy was home, we listened to *danzones* and *son montunos* played by El Sexteto Nacional y Sexteto Habanero on my father's state-of-the-art 78-rpm record player.

I attended kindergarten at PS 108, and then first and second grade at Santa Cecilia Elementary School, under the harsh Catholic discipline of the Sisters of Mercy and the Irish Christian Brothers. The image and the distinct sound of the rubber whips used by the teachers to inspire us kids to a higher achievement—and, of course, better values—are still vivid.

That was the 1950s, and I also remember the air-raid drills, preparing us in the event of a communist attack. During those kindergarten drills, students were meticulously trained to go under our desks to protect us from the bombs that were expected to fall all over the city. As five-year-olds, no one questioned these things. Much later in my life, the word "communist" would become meaningful in a very different context. For me and the rest of the kids in our neighborhood, the matter was quite simple; we were living in the times of the Red Menace. Communists were atheists who would destroy our way of life and would not hesitate to brainwash all of us and submit our whole society to a dictatorial regime. Everybody would be subjected to misery forever. Moreover, the communists would not even give many of us the possibility of yielding to their dominion: Most of us would die first, incinerated by the nuclear blast from the missiles that Russia would launch at every major United States city.

There was also the perceived internal threat. Communists could be anywhere and everywhere. Much later I would learn about the unwarranted repression and persecution of some of the United States' most valuable intellectuals and artists, as well as civic and labor leaders; how the FBI had become an instrument of repression of Native Americans, African-Americans, Puerto Rican nationalists, and everyone else who tried to fight for social justice or even simply affirm their identity in this country.

The streets were getting more violent every day, bloodied in gang warfare. My mother was growing increasingly concerned. It didn't feel safe to walk to the bodega. The Dragons, the Viceroys, and the Red Wings were street gangs that claimed turf in El Barrio, and each was a zealous guardian of the boundaries that separated Puerto Ricans from the Italian and other neighborhoods across Fifth Avenue. I was too young to know the gruesome details of all this, but I can remember my mother insisting that we should move to a better neighborhood. "El Barrio," she said, "is becoming a war zone."

The summer when I was four, we all went to Puerto Rico, to visit my grandmother. The trip was significant for me, and is one of my earliest memories. I threw up during the entire ride in the four–propeller-engine plane.

Grandma was short, round, and dark, with long black hair. She wobbled from side to side in her *chanclas* (a slang word for "slippers") and cooked real Puerto Rican food all day long. I gorged myself throughout our stay on *criollo* (down home) cuisine. Our big meal was at lunch, usually noon, and then, with full stomachs, it was siesta time. It was all so wonderfully different from my days back in New York. At night, the soft, soothing whistle sound of the penny-sized *coquí* frog would lull me to sleep. Their unique symphony can be heard only in Puerto Rico; *coquíes* have never been sighted anywhere else.

Puerto Rico was a magical place. It smelled and sounded unlike anything else I'd ever experienced. There were so many things to feel and taste. Tropical fruits like *guanábana* and *guayaba*, could be eaten right off the tree. The *doña* next to my grandmother had a thriving *limber* business. *Limbers* became a favorite

treat. The juice and pulp of any fruit was mixed with water and
sugar and poured into ice-cube trays. Each square was a *limber*
and for two pennies I could buy one. I had to eat it fast, otherwise it would melt under the hot Caribbean sun.

I was sorry to leave—even more because it meant having to
get on an airplane again. In the midst of a late August hurricane
my family and I flew back home. Buckets of water splashing
against the windows, the wind tossing us about, I vomited nonstop. We all made it home safely, but I didn't get on a plane
again for fifteen years.

A year after our trip to Puerto Rico, Mom decided to move the
family north across the Third Avenue Bridge, into the South
Bronx, an "upscale" neighborhood. Irish, Italians, Germans, Polish, and Jews lived in the underdeveloped borough where
pheasant-hunting still went on until the early 1960s. This was
the perfect neighborhood for an aspiring middle class family to
reside, preparing to send their children to "good" schools and
receive the education the parents had forfeited for economic survival. Ours was the second Puerto Rican family to move into a
"nice area" in the South Bronx: 988 Tiffany Street, between
Westchester Avenue and 163rd Street. It was a different world.
Our neighbors spoke only English and went to synagogues instead of Catholic or Pentecostal churches, and the grocery store
across the street closed every night before sundown. There
wasn't the street noise of our old neighborhood, although that
didn't last too long. A few years later, a wider trend began to
develop. It was as if a large number of people from my old neighborhood had followed us.

There was a plan—championed by Puerto Rican–born politician Herman Badillo, who had been appointed Commissioner

of Relocation by Mayor Robert Wagner—to end the over-
crowding in El Barrio by encouraging Puerto Ricans to cross the
Harlem River and move to the South Bronx. Under Badillo's
influence, large areas of the Bronx became Latino neighborhoods. That endeavor also served as a launching pad for Badillo's
political career; he went from being the first Latino borough
president (of the Bronx) to the first Latino member of Congress
in just a few years.

Our own family hoped to be recognized as middle class and,
looking back, my father's "reputable" job kept me away from
trouble in the street. In addition, both of my parents kept insisting on the importance of education for me and my sister. My
father often said that education was "the best gift a young person
could ever get from society." The hopes of my parents notwith-
standing, ours was just another blue-collar family. My father received pay for his labor, but we still lived from paycheck to
paycheck. When my father was abroad in strange and distant
seas, Mom would receive a check every fifteen days. Another
source of occasional income was my father's "private cargo directly from Spain."

When the money didn't arrive on time, my mother, my sister,
and I would kneel in front of the statue of La Virgen de la Caridad del Cobre, and pray. Since her early childhood my mother
had honored the patron saint of Cuba. When she was very
young, her brother Félix had attempted to light a kerosene stove
and accidentally set the house on fire. My grandmother ran to
her altar where she kept on display a towel-sized linen cloth with
the image of La Caridad del Cobre. As she ran outside of the
house she stopped and threw the pennant back declaring, "The
Virgin will save our house." La Caridad did, and my grandmother bought chains and medallions to be worn around the
necks of all her children. Today, four of her remaining children,

and many of her grandchildren and great-grandchildren, still carry on the tradition in gratitude to La Caridad del Cobre—"for saving our families' life and home."

The private religious ceremony in days of scarcity had an earthy aspect that I still remember with good humor. In our religious culture, it is customary to surround the statue with copper pennies as donations. My parents would empty their pockets daily and offer their change as a serious tribute to the heavens. When we had to endure those days of my father's paycheck being late, Mom would ask the statue for loans. "We're going to borrow some pennies from you today," she would tell La Caridad. "But don't worry, when Daddy's check arrives, we'll put it right back in the shrine. Okay?" The loan was approved every time. La Caridad's loan most often was enough to be eating fried eggs on top of white rice, or tuna fish with mayonnaise. We were aware that the Virgin's heavenly charity was not designed to enrich us economically, it was to teach us about humility and faith. Later, when the paycheck finally arrived, Mom would cash it and change the dollar bills into pennies to put back where they belonged, with the Saints.

While many other kids in my neighborhood joined street gangs or messed up their lives with drugs, I didn't: I felt safe under the sober protection of the Virgin. Of course, La Caridad del Cobre had a very powerful ally since my mother would have beat me if I ever brought shame upon the family. Besides, most of the kids in my neighborhood grew up either with a single parent, or with both parents working all day in order to have a chance at a decent life. I was lucky to have a family watching over me. There were other lessons life provided me. Among them were a sense of justice, and the will to fight oppression, and to overcome my own limitations and shortcomings.

This new life in the Bronx was about to propel me into a

lifelong journey of forgiveness and reconciliation. Tiffany Street—and what happened to me there before the age of eight—has been burned into my memory for eternity. It was there I suffered sexual abuse for the second time in my short life. Such an experience has the potential to scar the soul and to prevent any human being from having normal psychological development. Such an experience interrupts the natural development of the emotional self. I became aware of sex at an early and inappropriate age. My life became full of anxiety from the secret I kept inside of me. I became disconnected and detached from the people around me, a trend that would continue well into adulthood. I didn't trust anyone, especially adults. Thankfully, the negative consequences of that trauma have been offset by many years of therapy and the caring love of a safe family environment.

But pain and anger are difficult to overcome, and, occasionally, memories of abuse may have the power to incite feelings of despair. Pain can serve another, more positive function. I've found it can be a path to wisdom.

Physical, political, or economic rape is, fundamentally, about power. It is the innocent, trusting child betrayed by an adult, or an abusive boss taking advantage of a female worker or the developed military nation looming over the humbleness of a people; the outright theft of the natural and human resources of one society, for the economic, political, and military advancement of an empire. All of these are cases in which power is exercised to oppress. I'm sure the rage and anger I suffered in early childhood was channeled into my resistance to the oppressive forces bent on trampling the Puerto Rican community.

If abuse suffered at the hands of others gave me an early understanding of the dynamics of power, my dyslexia—undiagnosed for many years—created an empathy for people who are challenged, and gave me firsthand knowledge of how powerful human ingenuity can be. I was an outstanding student in history, social studies, and physical education, but horrible at reading and mathematics. It wasn't until I started Queens College that my dyslexia was discovered and I could finally deal with it.

To overcome pain and disability sensitizes us to justice. Many abuses stem either from lack of concern for other people's welfare, or from profit-motivated greed—often both. Fighting and defeating injustice is a very different type of experience; one you must be willing to pay a price for.

I first learned this when I was attending fifth grade at Public School (PS) 20. I had decided to stand up for a friend who was not ready to confront the class bully, Steve. I couldn't tolerate the continuous harassment and intimidation my friend was subjected to every single day.

All I remember about Steve was that he was white and had done some boxing. One hot afternoon, we came out into the yard, to engage in the first fistfight of my life. As it turned out, it wasn't really much of a fight. I hit the ground as soon as one fist connected with my mouth. I heard an awful sound: my jawbone cracking. When I finally staggered up, I had never felt so dizzy in my entire ten years of life. People—including my mother—quickly broke up the mismatch. It was one of my most embarrassing moments. What was I thinking, standing up to this guy, knowing absolutely zip about fighting?

My mother would pick me up every day at lunch and we would go to my *titi* Clara's house two blocks away for recess. On this day it was decided that I wouldn't go back for afternoon classes; instead, I was to spend the early afternoon getting instructions that became lifelong lessons for me. The first was how to defend myself with my hands, blocking punches, and how to move out of danger. I remember my mother and me bobbing and weaving in *titi*'s living room, training like boxers as I tried to learn the fundamentals of hitting with my fists and getting away from ripostes.

We must have been a sight. My mother is a delicate and gentle woman. She's quite short at five feet tall, and has a deceivingly fragile appearance. But she certainly knows how to defend herself. Championship fighters always say that in hand-to-hand combat it's not the weight or the stature, or even the brute force that determines the outcome of a match, but brains, character, and strategy. My mother has all three of these qualities in spades. That afternoon was a revelation for me. I knew, as any other kid would, that my mother was an expert in everything. To learn that she knew about boxing . . . well, that was really something! Boy, was she fast! Forearms and fists moved, highly coordinated and with decisive speed, to block and derail my attempts to pass her defense. Her feet were firm on the floor but still changed position so that the punches that could not be blocked by her arms would not hit their target either.

At the beginning of the training session, I felt weak, impotent. My fists did not carry strength at all. My movements were dumb and my attack lacked resoluteness. Mom was not going to let me stay that way. She encouraged me to continue. She ordered me to fight, to let my inner force fuel my fists. As the class went on, I began to get involved, to forget about my fear, and to focus on the attack and defense. All of a sudden, like in a game when a kid plays make-believe, I was completely in the fight. I was a fighter!

There was a lot more to it than the excitement of the physical training. She kept telling me about the importance of character and will—the ability not to be intimidated, under any circumstances, by your opponent.

No matter what, I'd decided to go back the following morn-

ing and face Steve, to even the score "by any means necessary."
It was my mother's motto: "In a conflict, you either win or you
lose." She pronounced those words long before the great Malcolm X preached on the streets of Harlem. I wanted to beat this
bully in the worst way. The next day I would go to school pet-
rified. I knew I had to rise to the occasion—or at the very least,
not embarrass my mom or myself again. I was determined to
face Steve, sore jaw and all.

I was scared stiff. I had to face this guy the morning after he
had knocked me on my ass. The truth of the matter is that I was
more terrified of my mother's wrath than ten guys like Steve put
together. So I paid close attention to her. The second lesson my
mother taught me was, "Whatever situation you find yourself in,
be creative and courageous enough to find a way to be victorious—especially if you feel justice is on your side." Another thing
my mother always told me: "Get to the battlefield before the
enemy." So I woke up early. There was no use in trying to sleep
late, since I'd been tossing and turning all night in anticipation
of the challenge.

I walked to school that morning almost in a trance. As I advanced slowly toward the building, my mother's words sounded
in my mind. I can't say my steps were resolute, I just kept putting
one foot in front of the other, without hesitation. I practiced
tensing my muscles and my feet. I had no idea how I was going
to defeat him, but I was sure that I would. Getting there first
would make all the difference.

At last I made it to the front of the school. I was alone; no
one else arrived at school this early. So I just stood there, slowly
looking in all directions, surveying the surroundings like a feline
predator. I remember trembling and furrowing my brow. At that
moment I felt like a panther.

After ten to fifteen minutes, I spotted him coming down

Simpson Street. By this time there was a small group of students and classmates outside the school's entrance. Everyone knew why I was there, and they all wanted to see if Steve would knock me on my ass again.

It was obvious he knew what was up. He walked with a long stroll, his fists already clenched and his face a fiery mask. I thought to myself: *He's coming late!* I had taken the battlefield before my enemy. Don't ask me why that minor aspect was so important for me, but somehow because of that, I knew he was already defeated. Fear was not controlling me. I was just eager to start the fight. Just a few more feet, and I could let him have it.

Steve got close, and as I roundhoused at him, he quickly put me in a headlock. His strong arms surrounding my neck left me with no space at all to maneuver. Both of his arms had me locked at his waist. I was breathless. My purpose was to attack, and attack I did. Not knowing a rapid release from a headlock, I attacked his face. Without thinking, the panther in me turned my hands into savage claws. When we were finally pulled apart, he was covered with scratches and blood. I was unscathed. The poor boy was stunned. He had lost his confidence. He had been defeated in public!

I never had another incident with Steve or anybody else at school. I guess whoever beats up the school bully becomes untouchable in the minds of the rest of the students. From that experience I learned that when you think you are unquestionably battling on the side of righteousness, your desire and commitment increase, as do your chances for success.

In 1959 I started seventh grade at St. Athanasius, on Tiffany between Simpson Street and Southern Boulevard. There were plenty of smiling white faces. The overwhelming majority of my classmates were Irish, Italian, German, and Polish Catholics. However, among the very few Latinos at that school, there was a young boy named Ronnie Puente, a seventh-grader who played the piano while perched on telephone books so that he could reach the pedals. He played at the weekly assemblies and at the annual Easter and Christmas shows. Ronnie became one of the five closest friends I had at that school . . . all Puerto Ricans except for one, Charlie Young.

I was mesmerized by the way Ronnie played the piano. Music has a unique soothing and restorative power that touched me immediately. I can't imagine a world without music, a world without musicians. My sister would play the piano we had at our apartment. When she or Ronnie played, I felt for the sounds. Years later, as a music promoter, I would hire the Tito Puente Orchestra and Eddie Palmieri to play at the Riverside Plaza Hotel. The prominent Puerto Rican mambo bandleader Tito Puente was Ronnie's father.

Catholic-school discipline, corporal punishment, was at times extreme. I was no stranger to a certain amount of physical discipline; it was just one way my own parents told me that some kinds of actions had consequences. It certainly was not vindictive or frequent. I was not afraid of my parents. I *was* afraid of Sister Acquinn. I learned about a new kind of fear from her. During my first days at St. Athanasius, I learned that Sister Acquinn, of the "Sisters of Charity," was the queen of corporal punishment. At one time or another we all felt the two-handed slaps that were launched from folded arms. Like lightning, before you had a chance to wink, both her left and right hands would land flat on both sides of your face. I learned many valuable things at St. Athanasius, including discipline.

The transition from four years in public school to parochial school was difficult enough. Trying to fit in as the new kid in class, academically and socially, also had its challenges. Perhaps it was my fear, not respect, of Sister Acquinn that blocked my ability to learn anything. As a result, I was left back in the seventh grade, only to get Sister Acquinn again when I went to the eighth grade the following year. Remaining close to her meant that my troubles at school would continue.

There was something more to Sister Acquinn than her merciless discipline. She was also a *very* good teacher. She knew how to explain things well—and overall, she was one of the best teachers I ever had. The sweet-and-sour memories I have of Sister Acquinn have made me realize that people with severe problems or shortcomings, like my dyslexia, should not be underestimated or discarded. The system of "zero tolerance" often means throwing away people who fail, without considering that all of us will eventually come up short in one way or another. Healthy societies should strive to educate people who are physically or emotionally challenged rather than discard them.

At the end of my eighth-grade year, in 1962, Sister Acquinn graduated me with honors and presented me with the school's Spirit Medal, given to the student most active in school affairs and fund-raising for commencement activities. She and I had learned to work together in peace, in the process developing a relationship that made me a better person, more than just a good student.

During my second try at the seventh grade, I'd joined the social scene at the church through the Catholic Youth Organization (CYO), and I took classes in Latin as preparation for becoming an altar boy, thought to be the first step toward entering the priesthood. I learned the opening of the Catholic Mass, *ad deum qui laetificat juventum*, fast enough to be paired up with Charlie Young for our first Sunday mass together.

He was a typical Irish kid from the South Bronx, of average height—stocky and so fast on his feet that he could box you out on a basketball court. We became good friends instantly; I think it was our sense of humor. And like every good altar boy, we shared equally the (purposefully, I think) leftover wine from the church services. I always thought it was an old recruitment trick on the part of the Diocese for every priest to leave out a little wine for the altar boys.

On Saturday-afternoon weddings, the best man of the bridal party would tip the altar boy a dollar or two. We would make enough money to go to the movies on Sundays. I remember enjoying *West Side Story* and *The Ten Commandments* for about 50 cents each. In those early days when I began to enjoy films by myself, I fell into the habit of bringing my mother half of my Bit-O'-Honey candy bar after the movies.

Most of the guys on the block were in the Boy Scouts but my overprotective mother wouldn't have let me out of her sight long enough to go on their field trips, so I never joined. Instead I enlisted in the Sea Cadets, which met every Thursday night at PS 75, a fifteen-minute walk from Tiffany Street. I was proud to wear the Navy uniform; ships were my father's workplace. In the Cadets we pledged allegiance to the U.S. flag and studied Navy lingo and marching formations. There were battalion meetings in other schools and communities. Once a year, all the Sea Cadets throughout the city would meet at the 67th Street armory and compete in marching exercises. Each battalion also presented their marching band. I played a single snare drum in the best Sea Cadet band in the city.

My life was slowly taking shape. I was becoming a man of

uniforms, donning either an altar boy's gown or a military fatigue. But I didn't end up as a priest or in the Navy.

I never wore a U.S. military uniform and there was one person who, without even trying, showed me that the priesthood was not my path.

I still remember her.

Elaine Segarra was in my new class and she was quiet. I was self-conscious whenever she was around. Too self-conscious. Is that what they call "puppy love"? There was an irresistible adolescent attraction between Elaine and me. We became friends, and through her I met Augie Mas, Bobby Cruz, Mikie Sanchez, and Eddie Cruz. The six of us became an inseparable cluster, indivisible, always looking out for each other. Most of us went to the same school, lived in the same neighborhood, and on Saturday nights after playing stickball, football, or softball, we'd go over to Augie's and listen to doo-wop. It was a golden time, and these were some of the best friends I've ever had.

My sister once had to take me on a date with her boyfriend Hiram, who later became her husband. I hated being a tag-along about as much as my sister did, but in this case it was a treat. We went to a live Sunday Matinee at the Apollo Theater in the center of Harlem, to see Frankie Lymon and the Teenagers, and my all-time favorite, the Heartbeats.

My love for music was becoming eclectic at an early age. At home my father listened to Cuban classical music of the 1920s, 1930s, and 1940s. My sister would listen to rock and roll and the music of a very young Charlie and Eddie Palmieri, also Johnny Pacheco, Pete Rodriguez, and of course the three great Palladium bands of Machito, Tito Rodriguez, and Tito Puente. During the four years I had spent in public school, once a month at assembly we were treated to what was called "(European Classical) Music Appreciation." I even liked that.

I divided my time between music and athletics. I thought it was a great combination and lots of fun. I joined the CYO basketball team. My first practice provided the first (and lasting) lesson in sports equipment and apparel. My boxer shorts were hanging out of my basketball shorts.

"Hey," the coach said, "you can't play if you don't wear a jockstrap."

"What's that?"

"A support that holds you in safely," said my coach Jack Lyons. I rushed home, cut out the inside of a bathing suit, and wore its inside lining as a jockstrap. Georgie Torres from the starting team told me it would be much better if I went to a sporting-goods store and asked for an athletic supporter. It was a leap into adolescence. Thank God I cleared that up at age eleven.

Yankee fever hit the Bronx in summertime; I was always more of a baseball fan than a player. A short bus ride from my block, my friends and I would spend many double-headers in the house that Ruth built, Yankee Stadium. I saw those great Yankee teams in the late 1950s and early 1960s, featuring Mickey Mantle, Roger Maris, Whitey Ford, Elston Howard, Yogi Berra, and the great manager Casey Stengel. And, above all, a great relief pitcher from Puerto Rico: Luis "Tite" Arroyo. Whitey Ford would have been just another pitcher without Arroyo's relief assistance.

Almost all of us memorized the statistics of our favorite baseball players. We could rattle off who was the leader at stealing bases, who had the highest batting average and the most runs scored—with lots of seemingly unimportant trivia thrown in for good measure. We also learned a lot about running—away from gangs, that is. We lived in "Crown" gang territory, bordering on Knights and Sinners turf. One of the reasons my family had left El Barrio was because of gang activity, and here it was again, back on the block. Gang membership was determined simply by your address. Venturing outside the territory often meant getting a beating.

Here also, though, was time for fun. During summer nights it was "Ring-o Leveo," "Hot Piece and Butter," "Johnny on the Pony," and "Kick the Can"—games from a different era. It was also the season for coconut and guava ice cream and other Puerto Rican delicacies—among them, most cherished was the "*piragüa*," shaved ice with fruit-flavored syrup.

Upon seeing the *piragüa* cart someone always screamed: "Time out!" The man pushing the small three-wheeled cart with a huge ice block in its middle would smile, pick up his ice scraper, and start to shave ice, put it in a paper cup, and then sprayed it with heavy syrups of strawberry, coconut, guava, or *tamarindo*. These moments were the fun components of the inconsistent and contradictory life of the poor in our neighborhoods. We always seemed to be balancing between good and bad, danger and pleasure, intellect and emotion.

Winters were always too cold, and our block too silent. Once snow started to fall, the mood of teenagers was energized two-fold. The fun would begin with snowball "wars" and end in racial insults. Inevitably the whole thing would end up in fistfights. It was always one side of a street against the other. The reward was simply the right to say: "We kicked your ass during the last snow-storm." This yearly event had become part of our subculture—winters were confrontation time; snow the weapon of war. I spent my early youth in the South Bronx between study and discipline, religion and sports, play and work, love and confrontation. The time was ripe for learning some serious realities about prejudice, discrimination, and injustice against the African-American community. I didn't learn about these things from the whites in my neighborhood. These sad lessons would come from my own people.

In the summer of 1962, my mother decided to take me to Tampa to visit my namesake uncle, Ernesto, the only one of the Avalos who'd missed the migration up north with the rest of the family. It took us twenty-two hours by train. My family lived on Columbus Avenue, right across from where "Have a Tampa" Cuban cigars were manufactured. I visited all my Avalos relatives living there including my cousins Gloria, Tony, Gilda, and Joey. The morning of the first Thursday we were there, we woke up ready to have fun just like we had done on Monday, Tuesday, and Wednesday. We had already established a routine: first we would get a Cuban sandwich at the restaurant next to the Cascade Pool, then visit the amusement park nearby, and finally jump into the swimming pool. I innocently suggested going to the pool. My cousin Joey said we couldn't go.

"Okay," I said. "Let's head up to the Ritz Theater on Main Street." The answer was no again. "Wait a minute," I said, laughing, not knowing how serious he was. "Why can't we go anywhere today?"

Joey looked embarrassed and said to me: "On Thursdays the Negroes have access to the swimming pool, the amusement park, and the movies."

"What do you mean?" I asked in disbelief.

"Well," Joey quipped facetiously, "that's the only day provided for them to have fun around here. The other six days belong to the rest of us."

I started to laugh, again convinced he was kidding.

"It's not a joke," he said firmly.

"If that's the case, then where do we belong?"

"Come on!" my cousin responded. "Most of us are light-skinned. What do you expect? Of course we share the six-day fun-time with the *blanquitos*."

I still wasn't sure if I should believe my cousin. It seemed unreal, a despicable situation, difficult to comprehend, for a Christian boy who believed that we really were all equal under the eyes of God and, of course, the United States Constitution.

Sure, I noticed differences in people's skin color, language, ethnicity, and religion. I hadn't known there were policies like this which could divide us and provoke serious confrontations. *Wouldn't the African-Americans be angry?* I asked myself. They were being discriminated against in the very place they were born. I'd heard Cubans say not-too-friendly things about black Americans, but I didn't realize they had been racist remarks. I commonly heard expressions in Ybor City like "piece of black rag," or, "The bogeyman scares children but blacks scare the bogeyman."

That Thursday was the first time I became truly aware of racism.

The next day we returned to the swimming pool. A sickening chemical smell hit me across the face. Nauseated, I complained about the heavy stench.

"What in hell is this?" I asked. "What is this disgusting odor?"

My cousin laughed as he walked toward me and started to pat me on the back. "Sorry," he said smiling, "but I can't answer that question. You're too sensitive for me."

"Come on, man," I said seriously. "What is this?"

"It's chlorine," he finally said. "The people in charge wanna make sure to rid this place of the tiniest smell, or awful bacteria Negroes may leave around on Thursdays."

"Come on, man," I responded again. "I'm serious."

"Yes," my cousin said, shaking his head in disgust. "So they make sure to obliterate any trace of that smell every single Friday morning." He knew it wasn't right and so did I.

There was no room in my mind for doubt. This was obviously a situation that went far beyond skin color, and although I was too young to comprehend all the implications, I suddenly felt the type of humiliation and dishonor blacks had been subjected to from the first day they arrived in North America. When I mentioned my feelings to my family, they assured me that, unlike New York, this was just the way things were in the South.

Those experiences in Ybor City opened new doors in my brain, and a wound in the center of my heart. This was the true beginning of my own knowledge about the tentacles of racism and outright discrimination constraining blacks and other "minorities."

My feelings went beyond anger, though. I began to wonder what role skin color, place of birth, gender, and language played in all of our lives. Once I learned that there were humans who disliked, hated, and killed others because of those distinctions, I thought something was severely wrong with the human race.

Rage was growing in me. How could I get rid of that destructive impulse? Many intelligent and sensitive people have been destroyed by rage. When resentment turns into rage, no level of destruction is enough, and the very foundations of society are at stake. You don't need to go to school in order to learn such things. Rage is also an understandable result of witnessing or being subjected to severe injustice. To ignore the reality of such a feeling is not the answer. Rage can be understood as a symptom of moral awareness, as a wake-up call coming from one's conscience. How to turn that anger into a creative and positive impulse in the struggle for a more decent and fair society, is the true challenge, a lifelong quest.

Of course I can say that now, after many years of dealing with the problem. Back then, however, I was too young to understand. I had a long way to go. At St. Athanasius I had learned that fascism and communism were narrow-minded political beliefs practiced by foreigners and strangers living in Germany, Japan, Russia, or China—countries whose philosophies were in direct opposition to the democratic system of the United States. To destroy those misbegotten ideas was the duty of all good, God-loving people in America.

Then, as I digested that philosophy, I was overtaken by the basic question: Why do some Americans hate other Americans simply because of their skin color, religion, language, or birthplace? To me that was unacceptable and hypocritical. After all, I'd always felt that people were entitled to be of every faith, national origin, gender, and political belief in America, and had even died to protect the best interest of the U.S.A. in every war "our" country had been involved in. To respect our basic differences and to coexist cordially, was a credit to our humanity. Besides, we were constantly made aware of our enemies, where they resided, and how to straighten them out: Korea, Vietnam, Santo Domingo, Panama, Grenada, and Cuba.

By the time I reached high school, I'd learned about some important elements of the civil-rights struggle. I had enough personal knowledge to give several arguments in front of the class about the lack of respect for these rights in America. I still had trouble comprehending why Irish, Italians, and Jews—who had white skin, thin noses, "good" hair, and spoke the language of the country—were also discriminated against by other Caucasians.

It was a complex issue, one that would force me to look even closer at the history of this country, particularly its founding. I didn't know much at the time—it would take years to weave a concise view—but this much was clear: Racism and discrimination in America went far beyond black and white.

The trip to Ybor City that summer before I entered high school became the genesis and cornerstone of my political consciousness. It would be four more years, though, before I would fully recall those Friday-morning pool experiences in Tampa— to try and understand and support the rage that erupted throughout the ghettos across the United States in the mid and late 1960s.

OPENING MY EYES

ALTHOUGH MY POLITICAL AND SOCIAL SKILLS developed early on, formal education was a struggle for me. School was definitely an acquired taste. I always felt much more comfortable at home than at school. Although I went to school only a few blocks away from home and the comfort of my mother, I remember feeling unprotected and vulnerable away from her. It was tough to connect with the other students, and my nervousness and self-consciousness only made things worse. Academically, the situation was just as bad: I couldn't seem to get the classwork done and had a hard time keeping up. School was a big playground as far as I was concerned, and therefore I messed up my grammar-school education—so much so, that instead of going to one of the more respected Catholic high schools like Mount St. Michael,

Cardinal Hayes, or St. Helena's, which my parents would have preferred, I had to start at Clinton High, a public school, in the fall of 1962.

I never matriculated at Clinton. Monsignor O'Brien, pastor of St. Athanasius Church, announced that Charlie Rios, Eddie Cruz, Charlie Young, Victor Morales, and I—all from the same neighborhood—would be given the unexpected opportunity to attend St. Agnes Boys' High School, the prominent Catholic high school in Manhattan. St. Agnes was a very small school, with only about ninety to one hundred graduates each year. It was located in a building on 44th Street, behind the St. Agnes parish, near Grand Central Station and not far from the U.N. building in midtown Manhattan. It didn't seem like the kind of school that would have to go looking for new students. But we knew better than to question Monsignor. This wasn't an offer. It was an order. He had five positions at St. Agnes and the five of us were the chosen ones, whether we liked it or not. I still don't know why Monsignor O'Brien included me on that list. I had failed, from an academic point of view, and was not a star in any sport. My mother probably had more to do with it than I did; she was very active in the parish, and I'm sure she had a quiet word about me with Father O'Brien on more than one occasion. Or maybe it was because I had been an altar boy at St. Athanasius and involved in the social activities of the church. I like to think Monsignor just saw something in me that no one else had, and decided to take a chance on me. I really don't know. What I do know was that my mother was proud and relieved that her Mikey was going to Catholic high school.

Since I didn't care much for school at the time, it was the idea of visiting midtown Manhattan five days a week that excited me. The first day of classes I went along with the other guys to the nearby Lexington Avenue subway station. We were all clad in our new St. Agnes uniforms and eager to start the most important part of the deal—the journey into "the City." Traveling downtown from the Bronx by ourselves gave us an intense feeling of independence. For the first time, we became familiar with subway stops beyond those in our neighborhood. This was the first time we had gone out on our own. We got on the train at the Hunts Point Station and it took us close to an hour to get to school on 44th Street. As we entered Manhattan, the voices around us started sounding different—people dressed and spoke with an accent unlike those in my neighborhood.

The school was four stories high with a cafeteria in the basement and a small basketball court on the first floor. I remember six classrooms per floor, adequate for such a small student body. Nobody seemed to know why it was called "the United Nations school," since there weren't any students related to the diplomatic corps. I don't recall ever meeting a foreign student there. It may have had something to do with the epoch: The United Nations itself was barely fifteen years old. The General Assembly building was quite new, and there was much enthusiasm over the fact that world representatives were meeting only a few blocks away. It was enough to give some sort of identity to the whole area.

I had no complaints about going to a Catholic high school, although the racial makeup of my class of 107 students included only three African-Americans and five Latinos. In fact, Class 1C was all white. Measured by standards established some years later, it could be said that we were the "token" minority students in the school, included in order to placate grievances from the African-American and Latino communities. Opening up only eight positions to minority students in a class of more than one hundred could be construed as discrimination. The fact is that the minority uprisings came later on. The standard of those days was set by the liberal ideals pervading the country, promoting the image of a good and compassionate America. It was the era of the Peace Corps and a liberal Catholic president, John F. Kennedy. My attendance at St. Agnes was a part of that vision.

However, the teaching staff of Marist Brothers was a less-than-compassionate group of men. They were the male version of the Sisters of Mercy from grammar school. The steady diet of corporal punishment and detention never waned, but Charlie Rios, Eddie Cruz, Charlie Young, Victor Morales, and I had been well trained in the art of surviving such a system. If that wasn't enough, we thought our tough outer shell of pride would protect us; we were Latino kids from the Bronx, and these middle-class *blanquitos* were not going to cheat us. At least, that's what we thought when we first crossed the doors of St. Agnes.

We quickly learned that no matter where we were from, we couldn't escape a tradition established long before we'd come to the new school. It consisted of ribbing, practical jokes, and mild hazing from the seniors who thought selling seasonal baseball and football game tickets to freshmen (a full semester's elevator pass with each purchase!) was a great way to make quick money. Needless to say, St. Agnes Boys' High did not have a baseball or football team and, worse yet, there *was* no elevator in the four-story building.

As a freshman I got hit in face with the vigorous academic program. Memorizing the Latin lexis of an altar boy was one thing; actually understanding and conjugating verbs were missions designed for linguistic geniuses, not for me. I had to construct sentences in Latin—and not just for the responses to Father Neil Connelly during Sunday mass. In the end, I managed to survive, but I can assure you, the Latin language and me never established good relations, though we are old acquaintances.

I never excelled in academics but had a great time as the sixth man off the bench on the basketball team. I was a forward, and if you left me unguarded I had a pretty good jump shot from the foul-line area. We were a small school destined to win the Division C title as a freshman team. Catholic high-school basketball teams throughout the city fostered many of the best players around, some becoming successful professional basketball stars. Charlie Young and I were on the court with greats like Lew Alcinder (Kareem Abdul-Jabbar) from Power Memorial, who went on to become the NBA's top scorer, and Dean Meninger, a former New York Knicks player who came from Rice High School. Others—like Felix "Lenny" Santiago from St. Helena's and Jose París from Rice, both distinguished as All-City basketball players—never had a chance in the NBA. They became outstanding players in Puerto Rico. Some of us were actually on the bench most of the time, but at least we were all in the same ball game.

Basketball remained my first love, but the summer before my sophomore year I joined the New York *Billikans*, a sandlot baseball team, as a backup catcher. Being a catcher seemed like the best way to be involved in every play of the game. Players like Carlos Rodriguez, Louie Valadroes, Raymond Rodriguez, and Sergio and Louie González, dominated, and Bill Ward was one of the greatest sandlot coaches of all time. We played doubleheaders on Saturday and Sunday mornings in a Bronx league. In the summer months we played in the Babe Ruth League with an additional two games a week in Babe Ruth Park, in the shadow of Yankee Stadium. I sat on the bench behind Louie and Sergio González, the Barrio brothers from Cardinal Spellman High School who were outstanding hitters and exceptional fielders. They threw their arms out cutting down second-base stealers, and were relegated to the outfield, giving us benchwarmers the opportunity to get into the game.

Louie and Sergio excelled in school as well as on the field, earning top honors at one of the toughest Catholic high schools in New York. As brilliant as they were, they always spoke about a cousin from Brooklyn, "primo Juan," who they thought was the brightest in the family. In the years to come, I would learn personally just how brilliant "primo Juan" was. Back then, he was only a legend.

Those sometimes distant "living legends" influence us more than we often know. The mind of a child is always downloading experiences, lived or imagined, into the hard drive of his consciousness. That way, we build a library of references with which to understand and assess the myriad situations that will be faced in a lifetime. A child who learns about bravery, honor, hard work, and other admirable qualities from the examples of those around him or her, as well as stories of those who are less fortunate, gains important role models. These role models can provide a sense of freedom and possibility, as well as aid in overcoming difficulties. So when friends I admired, like Louie and Sergio, told me about their brilliant cousin, they provided me with a new role model, a new frontier. Was it possible to be that smart? The self-evident answer was yes. "Primo" Juan himself was irrefutable evidence.

Life being what it is, I never properly thanked Juan for being so helpful to me during those years by setting the bar high for my own achievement. We influence each other in so many unknown ways; we unintentionally became examples to others.

The second year of high school had something more in store for me than learning about good role models. It was the year my generation lost its innocence to the realities of the world. It was the year of learning how people we cherish as heroes may fall, may simply be shot to death. It was the year of the first severe blow to my still-developing social consciousness.

On November 22, 1963, I was getting ready for a Junior Varsity basketball practice when we got the news over the PA system from Brother James that President Kennedy had been shot in Dallas, Texas. Our school canceled every sport practice. I went home to a sobbing mother. Daddy was away in the high seas. Mom and I, along with the rest of the country, mourned our president's terrible death. The specifics were still shrouded in secrecy. We were all angry without a target. The first Catholic president, and "they" kill him. The assassination of hope would become routine in the years to come: Malcolm X, Robert Kennedy, Dr. Martin Luther King, Jr. Time and time again, the memory of the murder of John Kennedy would be relived.

It was the same year I ran away from home and landed in my childhood friend Bobby Cruz's house. For obvious reasons, Mom had been overprotective throughout the years. It had become overbearing and suffocating—my every movement had to be accounted for. I felt I had no freedom to hang out with the guys. I wanted to make a statement by leaving the house: that I was responsible and I could take care of myself, and above all, that I would not bring disgrace to the family. Bobby's mother, Rose, was well respected by Mom. I thought that staying there overnight would appease my mother some; I was responsible enough to go to Rose. Rose called my mother and told her I was safe. My mother agreed to come over in the morning. With Rose in the room I pleaded with Mom for understanding. At sixteen, I'd started to feel it was time to "cut the apron strings" and become my own person. I understood my mother's concern, and actually welcomed her sense of protection and her thoughtfulness. I was an adolescent looking forward to my inalienable rite of passage into adulthood. I thought that having control over my movements and my thoughts was part of that transition. Fortunately, thanks to Rose, an agreement was reached.

What a first night! There I was, lying in a bed that was not mine, in a home that was not mine, either. Somehow I felt more the owner of myself than I had the day before. I had traded in a world in which everything was already solved and taken care of, for a wholly new one in which I would be the architect of my own destiny. Of course, I was still under the eye of an adult. Rose was in charge. Of course, it was a minor step—I had embarked on a path to personal freedom. Even after the lights went off, I remained awake for some time. There was something flowing through me—more than a current—that made me aware, fully awake. Even the sheets on the bed felt different against my skin.

My mother had done more than just allow me to taste freedom in Rose's house. She had introduced me to the importance of work. Her strategy had begun even before I moved out. During that summer, before I entered my junior year, my mother had asked my *madrina*'s nephew, Albie Diaz, who worked as a Pilot boiler repairman during the week and as a promoter in the Latino dance business on weekends, to take me out with him to the clubs and show me the ropes. Albie was cool; he drove a brand-new red Ford Mustang. He became the big brother I never had. Mom knew about my love for music and thought this would keep me off of the streets and out of trouble. Too young to attend the world-famous Palladium on 53rd and Broadway, in Manhattan, I nevertheless got to see the great big bands—Machito, Tito Puente, Tito Rodriguez, Vicentico Valdés, Charlie and Eddie Palmieri, Richie Ray—from the dance floors of the Riverside Plaza, the St. George and Taft Hotels, the Imperial Gardens ("Colgate Gardens"), the 310½, the D'lira, and the "3-in-1 Club" in Brooklyn, where Ralph Mercado enjoyed his humble beginnings. Clubs and hotel dances dominated the Latino entertainment business.

Although my father inspired my love of Afro-Caribbean music

and taught me everything he knew, Albie was my mentor on the business side of the music scene. It looked like we were partying every weekend, but it took a lot of work to bring together a large dancehall event. There were the production details, from lights to sound systems, as well as the economic arrangements and the advertising. With Albie, I learned hands-on all of the practical aspects of the trade—and loved every minute of it. I felt like such an adult going with Albie to all of the different venues, promoting "Cameos," Albie's club. We'd run into many of the greats that I had only seen onstage, like Tito Puente who would always acknowledge me and remember me as "his son Ronnie's friend from the neighborhood."

Learning the trade was one thing, but above all I listened hungrily to the stories the musicians told. Hearing of their lives, the hardships they endured in the quest for success, the not-always-so-bright side of dealing with promoters, club owners, hangers-on, and life on the road, was like going to college. It's those stories, their legacy, that made up for the financial losses we often took, no matter how jam-packed and amazing a show had been.

September came much too quickly. Charlie and I were in the same class for the third year. That journey from the Bronx to St. Agnes so long ago, had sealed our friendship; we knew by now that our lives would be connected for a lifetime. We did almost everything together, including varsity basketball and getting into trouble. One of our most memorable mishaps came on St. Patrick's Day. We couldn't march in the parade that year because we both had detention and were forced to stay back at school. We weren't sad, though. In the past, when we'd marched, March 17th seemed to be the coldest day of the winter. Instead we decided to have our own little celebration. Before school that day we went to his home near the Hunts Point station. We entered the apartment, greeted his mother, and left with a small, mayonnaise jar. It was the best homemade Irish wine I had ever tasted. Sipping the wine on the train made it very difficult for us to make it to school. By the end of the day everyone in detention had their own opinion of Mrs. Young's brew, but between the pissing and barfing, we all knew it was potent. The most popular place that day at St. Agnes Boys' High was the bathroom. I am sure that the "Irish Christian Order" knew the celebratory decorum of the day, but no one said anything. At one point Charlie passed out in a bathroom stall. I woke him up, he washed his face, and we barely walked back to the detention room. He had the toilet seat imprinted on his butt for weeks.

That was the same year I began to study Tae Kwon Do under the great master, S. Henry Cho, just before big business took root in the art and commercialized it forever. To charge a fee in order to take a black belt test is routine today. In our day, such a transaction would be considered blasphemy. This was far from the days of my battle with the bully at the grade school. Tae Kwon Do opened for me a new way of thinking and being. It was not only about winning, not even about just fighting. The whole idea of martial arts has to do with the connection between the capabilities of the body and the values of the soul. Training was more important than the actual fighting. Watching your adversary was more important than scoring a lucky punch. Above all, you had to move fast, in complete control of your emotions. That was by far the more decisive factor in order to win than hitting hard. Sooner than expected, I excelled in forms and free style, becoming proficient in the arts. Martial arts gave me a sense of self-confidence, both physically and spiritually.

Back on the block, Tito, Rocky, Eli, and my childhood friend, Walter, formed a social club that they named the Plebeians Fraternity. Tito was Mr. Cool Breeze—he could do no wrong. He played timbales and would dismiss you in a minute if you said something stupid. He turned me on to Cal Tjader, Sonny Stitt, Horace Silver, and Nina Simone. Felix "Rocky" Flores was the impeccable dresser with the latest style and threads. Rocky was the artist; he sculptured and worked with gold and silver. He once made friendship rings for me and Elaine. Eli was white as paper, with more black mannerisms and sayings than black people themselves. He was calling all of us "niggers" long before it was adopted as an endearing term among friends. We became the youngest group of men to get involved in the Latin dance business in the mid-1960s.

One time we rented out the Colgate Gardens and featured the music of Cal Tjader, the Pete Rodriguez Orchestra Broadway, and the Latin Jazz Sextet, a local band from Clinton High School. Tickets were sold in advance for $2.75 each. The dance attracted over nine hundred people and was an overwhelming success. Most of us had part-time jobs, and this was extra money that came two or three times a year depending on the number of successful events we had. We split some of the profits and saved the rest for our next event. All of the dances were successful and in June of 1965 we expanded from a Bronx-only to a citywide dance. We had a big overhead to cover, at the Riverside Plaza Hotel, this time going into the big leagues with the dance music of the legendary—even back then—Tito Puente, and Eddie Palmieri. Inflation set in and the $3 mark was broken: advance tickets were $3.25, $5 at the door. Every record shop, from B&G Records on southern Boulevard to Casa Latina in El Barrio, sold tickets for 10 percent of sales. The success of these events depended on advance sales and a decent walk-up to the gate. Any good promoter has a good sense of the probability of success before the doors open. The promotion this time around had to be much more aggressive, and reach throughout the city. This meant going to every dance in Manhattan, the Bronx, and Brooklyn, a task we divided among the eleven members. It paid off. We made big money that night, and felt like we were part of the big leagues along with the Ralph Mercados and Albie Diazes of the day.

We were all Cal Tjader fans. Calvin Radcliff Tjader was a percussionist and played vibraphone, or the "Vibes." He was featured with pianist George Shearing, one of the first artists to record Latin jazz music. Latin jazz omits the Spanish lyrics of Afro-Caribbean dance music. As such, Latin jazz attracted a broader range of listeners. Many *blanquitos* and blacks, along with Latinos, were dancing to "Mambo Terrifico" and "Continental," two Tjader hits of the 1960s. When he toured the East Coast we were in charge of his "Last Appearance Before Departure to the West Coast" concert, one of the largest dance events ever. Although everyone sold tickets, I became the main promoter for the Plebeians. It was one of the most successful nights we ever had. I still remember Charlie working the room, saying that Cal was his uncle and he was doing the tour with him. The truth was, Charlie was the only white dude we let hang with us. He loved two cultures, his own "fighting Irish" tradition and our Latino salsa. He attended all of our dances and we renamed him "Paddy-Rican."

It wasn't all fun and games. The threat of going to Vietnam loomed. We were all a year away from having to register with our local draft boards. Body counts made front-page news and we all wondered if we would be next. None of us could articulate it, but many of us suspected that something was wrong with this war.

As we approached the end of our third year, my "puppy love" Elaine and I had grown apart from each other. She was very pretty, smart, and sensible, but we just grew up and became friends.

I began to notice another girl on the subway. She looked Puerto Rican but with a touch of something else I didn't recognize. The group (Charlie Young, Charlie Rios, and I) traveled together on the trains. Rios spotted a group of girls and was bold enough to introduce himself to one of them. Rios was interested in her but didn't follow up. I found out her name was Mutin Miah. She had two sisters (Doleza, Connie) and a brother in Puerto Rico. She lived with her mother, Aida, a woman from Naguabo, a small town on the northeastern coast of Puerto Rico, and her father was a native of what was then East Pakistan (Bangladesh)—probably the look that caught my eye. By her book covers I noticed that she attended Central Commercial High School on 42nd Street, two blocks from St. Agnes. We fell in love, and during a very hot June evening on an overpass near Hunts Point, I built up enough nerve to ask her to be my girlfriend. I didn't know what to expect, but she said yes with an unbelievable smile. In that instant my whole world changed.

Everything seemed to be changing quickly these days. The civil-rights movement exploded in the black community throughout the United States, led by El-Hajj Malik El-Shabazz (Malcolm X), and Dr. Martin Luther King, Jr. César Chavez was organizing migrant workers, Rodolfo "Corky" Gonzalez was representing "Crusade for Justice" in the Southwest, while Puerto Ricans Cha-Cha Jimenez and the Young Lords were gangbanging in Chicago. Jose "Chegüí" Torres had become the third Puerto Rican ever to win a world boxing championship. Juan

González, the living "legend" from Brooklyn thanks to the stories reported by my friends, made it to Columbia University. And I would graduate from high school in June 1966.

I went to work full-time that summer at Ripley's clothing store, joining my friends Walter Bosque and Joe Pérez. But it was just a short interlude. Adulthood had arrived, and along with it, the war. It stopped being a distant problem and became a very personal one. With the war effort escalating, the draft was breathing down hard on all our backs. In an effort to postpone induction until I could figure something out, I went to Whitehall Street and Fort Hamilton for a preinduction physical six times.

Eddie went to the Marines, Mikey to the Air Force, Bobby to the Army, while Augie attended St. Frances College. My neighbor, Pedro, came back in a body bag with his tags on his big toe.

It just didn't make sense. Was there any reason for him to die? The news on the TV, the radio, or the papers did not provide a good answer to that question. War was not popular. Neither was defeat.

So much has been written about the Vietnam War and the anti-war movement in the States during those years, it seems unnecessary for me to revisit that entire history. But certain things about that time ought to be remembered in order to understand the development of the Young Lords.

Nobody knew when that war started. Tons of paper were wasted trying to explain the difference between a "war" and a "conflict." There was not a war in Vietnam, but a conflict. Then how come Pedro was dead in a war that was not taking place? Human beings are the only animals that know the names of things. Maybe that is the reason why when the politicians in power fail to name things correctly, the people feel their intelligence is being assaulted and suspect a plot by the government. The suspicion was so widespread, that the mayor of New York,

John V. Lindsay, was among the voices against that war, and claimed it was draining the city of badly needed lives and funds just to please the military-industrial complex.

There was another aspect to it. The "enemy" looked too much like us—Puerto Ricans. American troops were destroying shantytowns in a remote country, which had an eerily similar appearance to the tropical country of our fathers. Either through the press or by the stories brought back home by the friends who survived their tours of duty, instead of tales of heroism we heard horrific and obscene recounts of mass murders, senseless destruction, and hell. The way in which the Viet Cong, a Southeast Asian David, armed with little and using bamboo boobytraps, were able to foil the high-tech American Goliath was encouraging.

There was also a very subjective matter: Respect. The war in Vietnam was not only considered a failure in itself but, unlike World War Two, those who were sent there did not have the respect or the praise of the community. To leave the Bronx clad in a military uniform was not a badge of honor.

The only way to stay out of the Armed Forces was to escape to Canada or become a student and receive a "2S deferment" which was granted by your local draft board. I did apply to a couple of universities when I finished high school, but I didn't get into any local colleges, and almost gave up the idea. I was scared shitless to come home from the war like Pedro.

Still, I had a crazy scheme, if it would only work. I'd joined the U.S. Air Force and didn't have to report to active duty for ninety days. This would give me enough time to take the Search for Education, Excellence, and Knowledge (SEEK) program entrance exam, a program aimed at helping students in need of remedial academic work, or in a low economic bracket, get into college. If all went well, I would receive my acceptance letter to the program, and to a college, before my ninety days were up. It came nail-bitingly close. After the sixty-day mark passed, I started to really panic at the possibility of spending four years in the Air Force. Finally, the letter arrived that would determine my future. I took a deep breath, asked Saint Jude to do what he knows best (which is the impossible), and opened the envelope: I had been accepted to the City University of New York (CUNY) at Queens College, the least integrated of all CUNY institutions in "lily-white" Kew Gardens, Queens. I can't even describe how relieved I was. I had been given another life and I knew deep inside me that this was a turning point.

As the summer went on and September approached, my relief became overshadowed by my growing anxiety as the reality of attending college sank in. I'd never even read a book cover to cover, and now college classes and professors loomed. I was going to have to work hard and take some non-credit remedial courses as well as classes for credit, but I believed in myself enough to know that I would do well. It seemed like heaven when compared to the alternative, and a necessary step toward gaining the respect of my family and community that I so wanted.

While I started college in the spring of 1967, Walter, Tito, Raul, and the rest of the Plebeians went from party to party: the Roundtable on Sunday, the Village Gate on Monday, Cheetah on Thursday, the Bronx Casino on Friday, and Arnie Segarra's Chez José on Saturday. There was a very good reason to party hard. These were the last few months the selective service would grant 2S deferments. Of course it was too good to last, and by the end of 1967 the Plebeians had broken up. The military draft seized some of the guys; others left for Puerto Rico to avoid the burgeoning drug epidemic. One out of five young people in the Mott Haven area of the Bronx was addicted to heroin. Walter and I were the only ones who went on to college. After splitting up the money we'd earned, we all went our separate ways.

On campus I felt self-conscious, but I knew I had to get through this academic plunge somehow. Black and Latino students were an obvious minority; we were for sure a new sight in the student lounge and cafeteria. We stuck together and didn't give a shit. We knew we had as much right to be there as anyone else, and we were just beginning to understand our rights and stand up for them. We reclaimed our right to have access to higher education, and eventually demanded and received black and Puerto Rican studies programs in every single CUNY institution.

The "SEEK students," as we were referred to with an air of disdain, organized our own political activities and rallies on campus. Sure, we wanted an end to the war, but we were also insisting on an end to colonialism in Puerto Rico, Africa, Latin America, and Asia. We also wanted social justice (education, housing, health care, full and equal employment) for all national minorities within the United States.

At one of those rallies I got a chance to see and meet a young poet reciting a poem entitled, "Jibaro, My Pretty Nigger." The title alone got my attention. The lines that still resonate went:

> "Jibaro, my pretty nigger. Sweating slowly to the strummed strains
> of a five-string guitar, remembering ancient empires of sun gods
> and things that were once so simple. Jibaro, my pretty nigger-man.
> Fish smells and cane smells and fish and cane smells and tobacco,
> and oppression makes even God smell foul . . . forget about self,
> we're together now . . . and I'll never let you go! Never, nigger!"

I was left with one of those chills that begins in the middle of your back and travels to your hairline.

After the poet had finished reading, I went up to him and introduced myself. Over the next couple of weeks I would learn that his name was Felipe Luciano and he had just gotten out of jail for manslaughter after getting mixed up in a gang fight in which a young man was killed. Physically well-defined and sporting an Afro with pride, Felipe had a genuine smile and incredible charisma. He spoke with uncommon knowledge and wisdom about sociopolitical issues. He had been reading and thinking in prison for two and a half years, and had formulated a very political and social persona. He could talk and persuade you with style and vocabulary, but there were times when he settled things with a left hook or a right cross. It was clear that Felipe not only spent time in the weight room but also had done more than shadow-boxing in the joint. He had been paroled and now attended Queens College.

After spending several months fighting for common causes on campus, Felipe and I became good friends. The spring semester of 1967 came to a close at Queens College. Although I survived that year and was returning in the fall, I did begin to question the Eurocentric approach to higher education. I was getting bored. That summer I kept up with Latin music and often went to social or dance clubs to meet up with old friends, reconnect with my community, and have a little fun. The news never let me forget about the turmoil and injustice wracking the world, and when it came violently into my own neighborhood, it would change my life forever.

The *New York Times*' front-page lead story on Monday July 24, 1967, was "Detroit is Swept by Rioting and Fires; Romney Calls In Guard; 700 arrested." And, when it was all over, forty-three people were dead. The riots also caused over $150 million in business and residential damages. But the headline that caught my attention was in the right-hand corner: "Disorders Erupt in East Harlem; Mobs Dispersed." The East Harlem riots erupted because two people were wrongly killed by police. Giving vent to years of frustration and disenfranchisement, residents of El Barrio took to the streets. As I read accounts of the riot along with the shocking state of the living conditions people were forced to endure in El Barrio, I took it very personally. I felt that I had been lied to for years and had finally found the truth on the front page of *The New York Times*.

The truth was clear to me: Puerto Ricans were not being treated as equals; that we were being denied the basic rights endowed to us by the Creator: life, liberty, and the pursuit of happiness. No, sir—the whole Declaration of Independence of the United States was a lie for the people of El Barrio. All this was happening to the neighborhood of my early years, where my parents had begun our family. It was a matter of respect. Rage, that old acquaintance from childhood, surfaced again.

I remembered that Louie and Sergio Gonzalez lived in the Carver Houses in the middle of El Barrio and I was sure that they would know what was going on. I called Louie, and he told me that city officials were looking for college students to come into the area and talk to young people in order to avoid any further disturbances or killings.

During 1966 and 1967, the word "riot" was commonplace in the city. Among those incidents, some of the most serious were the cases of East New York and other Brooklyn areas, as well as the garbage-burning uprising in the Bronx. The city, composed of a structure, like a quilt, had developed out of several ethnic communities and interest groups that barely communicated with each other. Above all, the wealthy class was rapidly developing into a white elephant, while poverty-stricken areas continued to deteriorate and became an ominous sign that most of the city could turn into a wasteland. More than a million New Yorkers lived on earnings that did not reach even the minimum required for monthly survival. African-Americans and Puerto Ricans had the honor of being the better represented in that group. Poverty by itself does not explain civil turmoil but, once it has begun, certainly serves as an endless source of fuel.

Mayor Lindsay's response was to create a citywide program for sending task forces to dozens of the most volatile neighborhoods. The idea was admirable—peacemaking—but it did nothing to radically change the system. Although the program was ineffective in the long term, at least the city administration was trying to pay attention to people's grievances. It provided many college students with a hands-on learning experience about community issues, and a stipend.

That summer I returned to El Barrio as a peacemaker. I worked with Louie on a project aimed at helping the youth of the community and met a group of people that helped change my political perspective. Arnaldo (Arnie) Segarra was an organizer for the East Harlem Tenants Council who, after the riots, was given a position within city government. Arnie had grown up in this community, left for college, and then returned. Arnie had recently opened the Chez José, New York's most elegant Latino nightclub, with a strict age and dress code.

I also met Angelo Giordani, Willie Vasquez, Harry Quintana, Victor Feliciano and Robert Garcia—all from the Real Great Society, "University of the Streets" (RGS)—at the First East Harlem Youth Conference, at Columbia University in August 1967, one month after the riots. RGS was the most progressive community-based organization in El Barrio because it recognized the emerging Puerto Rican nationalism and militancy being expressed by the young people. I was so impressed with the individual histories of these guys that I immediately wanted to join them.

Angelo was a well-known former Dragon who attended Harvard and Pace University where he graduated at the top of his class and then came back to the neighborhood. Willie was the organizer that everyone knew and trusted. Harry was an ex–drug addict who got clean and went to Howard University and became chairman of the student strike committee. He also returned to East Harlem.

It was from Harry's mouth that I first heard the name Don Pedro Alibizu Campos. We had all left El Barrio for different reasons, some willingly, others without a choice, but in some strange coincidence that only Providence can explain, we all found ourselves together at this moment in time. I became the newest member of RGS. I founded the East Harlem College Student Society, and developed mentoring and tutoring programs to help young people get into college and then hopefully return, much in the same manner that we had returned to give back to El Barrio, to share their talents with our community.

I returned to the QC campus that fall, feeling I had developed a cultural identity defined by my Barrio roots. Felipe and I began to have qualitatively different conversations. I was for the first time in my life experiencing the world as a Puerto Rican. I always knew I was ethnically Puerto Rican but after that summer in El Barrio I became politically aware of my pride in being Boricua. That winter I mainly went to school, worked at RGS, and dated Mutin.

The spring of 1968 was marked by a surge of student takeovers of campus operations throughout the U.S. to protest the war in Southeast Asia. Third-world students' takeovers often included the demand for academic programs to be relevant in the context of their lives, and less Eurocentric. The insistence for black, Puerto Rican, Asian, Native American, and women's studies became part of the demands that college officials had to respond and acquiesce to. I was becoming more interested and involved in the issues that affected Latinos on campus and in El Barrio. I was losing interest in school and beginning to fail in my classes. If I failed out, I would be faced with the possibility of being drafted again.

RGS and the University of the Streets' approach to community and education caught the attention of the planning committee at the State University of New York College at Old Westbury. The committee, headed by Harris Wafford, who eventually became a Pennsylvania senator, found its way to East Harlem to talk to us about education, life experience, and relevant field study. They were putting together a new college that would move away from the traditional Eurocentric approach to education. Somehow, again, what my mother would have called divine intervention, rescued me from the war in Vietnam. Competition would be steep for the less than seventy-five slots for the founding class of SUNY College at Old Westbury. I was accepted in March of 1968 and dropped out of QC to work full-time and prepare for the summer programs in East Harlem.

In April, New York became the stage for one of the most dramatic and bloodiest student takeovers in the country, and it occurred at one of the preeminent Ivy League schools: Columbia University.

The college wanted to build a new gymnasium with an Olympic-size swimming pool and a basketball court that would expand their sports recruiting program. The community was against the proposal. They felt that the plan was an encroachment on their recreational community space. The Black Student Union and the radical Students for a Democratic Society began to organize a student strike committee to block the college from building the gym. Juan González became the chairman of the student strike committee and was all over the news when students shut down Columbia on April 23. That day I headed to 116th and Broadway to find Louie and Sergio's cousin. We were having our problems in East Harlem. One year after the riots, city government denied funding for twenty summer programs. Umberto Cintrón from MEND (Massive Economic Neighborhood Development) and I organized thirty summer programs that received funding. We decided to reject the money until all the programs were funded. If there was not money for all, there would be no money accepted by the few. For us it was a matter of sheer fairness and a way to prevent the government from pitting us against each other in a stupid competition to win bureaucratic favor.

The burning rage that kept growing in me was yielding to experience in this summer community work and the need to develop a keen sense for unexpected political opportunities. I was learning how to take advantage of whatever resources were handy, or at least attainable. Memory thus played an important role. As soon as I learned that the famous "Primo Juan" was the leader of the Columbia University uprising, my mind went into a swirl.

I thought I could meet Juan and garnish support for our protest against the city. So, early on that April morning, the Harlem community went to Columbia University, and I went in search of Juan. There, on the steps of Leob Library with a red band around his left arm, I spotted Juan and went right up to him. "My name is Mickey Melendez, I know and played baseball with your cousins, Louie and Sergio, I'd like to talk with you." It wasn't the most graceful of introductions, but I knew my mere friendship with the González brothers would smooth things over. When he only nodded, I smiled and asked him, "What are you doing in the middle of the struggle with all these *blanquitos*?" The scene was chaotic, people everywhere, everyone shouting, and everyone trying to get Juan's attention. It clearly wasn't a good time for a chat, but we managed to exchange numbers. I called him two days later.

I told him about the struggle in East Harlem and our organizing efforts to get total funding for all the summer programs. Juan joined us and brought some radical *compañeros* from Columbia to help make some smart noise and block traffic on the East River Drive in order to bring attention to the abused community. City officials were forced to meet with the organizing committee in East Harlem and eventually came up with the money they had previously denied the community.

That summer Juan had two victories: the students at Columbia successfully halted the building of the gymnasium, and all summer programs were funded in East Harlem. The East Harlem College Student Society/RGS had received its summer funding in the first round. That summer I directed Project YEAH (Youth Education Among Harlemites) and had Juan come to speak to the young people in the program. We stayed in touch that summer as I prepared to enter Old Westbury in September of '68, with Denise Oliver who knew Harry from Howard University in D.C. and was a member of RGS, and Roberto Ortiz, a community organizer.

As soon as the summer program was over in late August, I went to Planning Fields in Oyster Bay. Fire had destroyed the temporary dorms at Old Westbury and we were rerouted to a three-hundred-acre arboretum with geodesic domes and a Japanese garden. Incoming students were encouraged to arrive on campus before the first days of class to help finalize a curriculum. To lure the students back on Sunday nights the college menu included a choice of a lobster or steak dinner with cherries jubilee for desert. Particularly for those of us that were part of the first class, Old Westbury was the most life-altering educational experience of our lives.

Of seventy-three students, only eleven of us were nonwhite. A small number of Latinos among the student body got together with Carlos Russells, an extraordinary Panamanian professor, and created a group called "the Non-White Caucus." All eleven joined. Carlos had interviewed Malcolm X years before his assassination. It was the closest we got to Malcolm. We read and discussed *The Brothers Karamazov*, *One Dimensional Man*, and *The Autobiography of Malcolm X*. Carlos looked like us and spoke into that vacuum that we all had been denying was our history. We liked Carlos because he was smart and had answers. He told us where to find the truth. Carlos left a mark on our political consciousness forever.

Paul Guzmán's room was down the hall. The six foot, three inch, lean, black young man appeared more African-American than Cuban–Puerto Rican. He had just graduated from Bronx High School of Science. I was totally impressed with him. He was clearly well-read, intelligent, and one of the most hilarious people I had ever met. Paul knew how to have fun all the time. He had the ability to find the absurd side of the sublime and make it comical.

Paul and Ron Batson's room was the music and party center in the dorms. We all congregated to the sounds of Iron Butterfly, Ten Wheel Drive, Bob Dylan, Otis Redding, and lots of beer. It was at one of those parties one day, that I left with Robert Bunkley to go to his room, and got high for the first time in my life. The red hashish had a distinct aroma and wonderful taste. A couple of hits from a pipe and I started to hear the cork in the ceiling crackle. I went out for a walk in the arboretum and felt a sense of euphoria. Not only was Old Westbury a long-lasting educational experience, it was the place where many of us got introduced to the drug side of the youth and cultural revolution of the 1960s. Getting high was as normal as going to classes on campus.

Paul and I got to talking about our family histories and found many similarities in our background: partly Cuban, New York–born, raised by a strong mother figure, a love of music. Most important, we both were searching for an identity and purpose in life. We both had heard of the Nationalist Party of Puerto Rico. From high-school history we understood that Puerto Rico had become a possession of the United States after the Spanish–American War—and that one day we had gone to sleep Puerto Ricans, and woken up U.S. citizens, without consulting the democratically elected legislative body of our government. We had vaguely heard about the Ponce Massacre of 1937. We also remembered something about an attempt on President Truman's life that coincided with the revolt of 1950 on the island, and that one Nationalist was killed and another was sentenced to life. We knew that four Nationalists had charged into Congress on March 1, 1954, unfolded a Puerto Rican flag, yelled out, *¡Viva Puerto Rico Libre!* and opened fire. What we didn't know was the politics of it all. We didn't understand the political background or history that had provoked those actions. I suggested to Paul that we go to the library and look up how these events had been reported in the printed media.

Late at night and partially stoned, we would make our way into the library and go to the microfiche and begin to pull up newspapers—*Journal American, Daily Mirror, Herald Tribune, Daily News, The New York Times*—and read the accounts of those events in our country. For weeks we kept asking ourselves, *Why?* Why did the United States invade Puerto Rico? Why did they make us U.S. citizens? Why did "the Americans" kill so many innocent Puerto Rican people in Ponce? Why? Why? Why? We were repeating the same questions that the anti–Vietnam War movement had injected into the consciousness of the United States. We had come across the answers because we asked the first question. The truth is found by first asking questions. All along there had been a suspicion that something had been kept from us. We unraveled a history that had been purposefully denied us as we grew up in "America." At last, we had found a history rich in courage and resistance. There was an old legend— and a new story to be told. We started to formulate our truth. There once were Taínos and Arawak warriors, indigenous people who fought the Spanish invaders and committed mass suicide rather than submit to a cruel life as slaves to the King and Queen of Spain.

Dr. Ramón Emeterio Betances—who led the struggle against Spain in 1868, for the abolition of slavery and independence for Puerto Rico—is recognized as the father of our country. History credits him with the development of free-thinking men and women with a vision of self-determination and sovereignty, like Ruiz Belvis, Luis Muñoz Rivera, and José Celso Barbosa, who provided a body of literature and a historical point of reference for generations. We learned more about the history of Don Pedro, the visionary man who returned to Puerto Rico at age thirty with a bachelor of philosophy, masters of sciences and arts, industrial chemist and civil engineer degrees from the University of Vermont, doctor of philosophy and letters and doctor of laws degrees from Harvard. We were astounded and very proud of the academic accomplishments of a *puro compatriota*.

This is the history that we proclaimed for ourselves, and we

My mom and dad, dressed for my baptism

My sister, Helen, in 1960

In my uniform: Seaman, second class, Sea Cadets

The Plebeians Fraternity (*left to right*): Freddie Sanchez, Walter Bosque, Victor "Tito" Rodriguez, Angel "Lefty" Ortiz, Al Cruz, Cal Tjader (*center*), Jules Asencio, Eli Irrazary, me, Raul Ortiz, Freddy "Rocky" Flores, Louie Valladares

A poster for one of our events

A rally at Tompkins Square Park in 1969. On stage (*left to right*): Georgie Garcia (former Viceroy), Herman Flores, Felipe Luciano, Gabriel Torres, Unknown, Pablo "Yoruba" Guzmán, Georgie Lemus (former Dragon). Lower level (*left to right*): Unknown, Tony Rosa, Carlos Aponte, Jose "Pi" Diaz, and me. *HIRAM MARISTANY*

After the hijack of the mobile X-ray truck. I'm on the far left, in the short-sleeved white shirt, speaking with Geraldo Rivera (back to camera). To the right of Rivera are Juan "Fi" Ortiz and Gil Noble (in the white suit and black tie). *HIRAM MARISTANY*

Walking across the 59th Street bridge in 1969 in protest
of the arrests of the New York Panther 21. I'm in the far
right corner with David Perez to my right. (*Left to right*):
Larry Louzu, Denise Oliver, Iris Benitez, Richie Perez,
Iris Morales, Lulu Cabera. *HIRAM MARISTANY*

With Denise Oliver dur-
ing the Lincoln Hospital
takeover. *HIRAM MARISTANY*

Last respects for Julio
Roldan, October 1970.
MICHAEL ABRAMSON

The front page of *El Diario/la prensa* on October 26, 1977, after our takeover of the Statue of Liberty. EL DIARIO/LA PRENSA

During the protest at the United Nations in December 1999. (*Left to right*): José Torres, Gladys Peña, me, and Luis Garden Acosta.
JOSE ROSARIO/EL DIARIO/LA PRENSA

With Rubén Blades at the protest.
JOSÉ ROSARIO/EL DIARIO/LA PRENSA

At an interview with "Panamá" at the offices
of *El Diario/la prensa* after the protest.
JOSÉ ROSARIO/EL DIARIO/LA PRENSA

Celebrating my fortieth
birthday (*left to right*):
Eddie Palmieri, Tito
Puente, Armindo Morales,
me, Arturo Ramos (*front*),
Felipe Luciano, and Israel
"Cachao" Lopez.
CALIXTO "COOKIE" ALVAREZ

My daughters, Ata-Celia and Haydee, with my granddaughter, Amina Kai

My son, Amilcar Dohrn-Melendez

My son, Miguel Albizu Melendez

One of my daughters' most prized possessions: an autographed photo of
Celia Sanchez and Haydee Santamaria with Fidel Castro during their
time in the Sierra Maestra

couldn't wait to tell others. We began to believe in the possibility that we could become an independent and self-governing nation, controlling our own economy and our own destiny. We redefined ourselves in this tradition of struggle and resistance against powerful foreign intervention; we embraced this history as our own. At that moment and without any hesitation Paul and I became revolutionary nationalists.

We started to watch how other national minorities—Mexicans, Native Americans, African-Americans—were raising their voices, and having massive demonstrations and protests, demanding social and political justice here and in the internal colonies of the United States. We knew Puerto Ricans should do the same.

As a people, we'd developed a colonial mentality: docile, subdued, and clutched with a profound self-doubt that destroyed our sense of self-worth and our confidence. Unlike most countries in South and Central America, Puerto Rico was constantly blocked from developing its own economic and political identity. As a result, we'd failed to protect our unique history from both the *españoles* and the gringos. It was time for that to change.

I was so excited about what I had learned, that I wanted to introduce Paul to Juan and Felipe (who visited Old Westbury and wooed everyone with his revolutionary poems and charismatic charm), so that we could discuss it further—and maybe do something about it. Felipe and Paul hit it off immediately. They were matched wit for wit. We went into the city to meet with Juan and again it appeared a perfect match. I'd brought together three of the most active, politically savvy, and intelligent young men I had ever met.

The college kept a pool of cars emblazoned with the New York State seal indicating they were "FOR OFFICIAL GOVERNMENT BUSINESS ONLY" on the grounds. On more than one occasion we

"appropriated" them to go to Bill Graham's Fillmore East Theater in Downtown Manhattan. I remember watching anxiously
as Paul scaled the geodesic domes into where the car keys were
kept. The risk was more than worth it. It was a mind-blowing
experience to see for the first time in person, bands and individuals like: Big Brother and the Holding Company with Janis Joplin, Buddy Miles, the Byrds, Santana, and many more. Paul
turned me on to the Fillmore and it became a weekly event for
months.

By now Paul had become an expert dome-climber. At one
point, we learned that the pro-statehood governor Luis A. Ferré
of Puerto Rico was coming to New York. At once, we started to
organize some of the students to go into the city and demonstrate against the idea of statehood. Paul got the government
automobiles and filled them up with students. We then traveled
to the Waldorf Astoria to demonstrate against the governor of
Puerto Rico, the strongest supporter for making the island the
fifty-first state, who was staying at the famous hotel.

Two days later, we were called into the dean's office where
we were shown photographs of Paul and me getting out of two
of the university's official automobiles. Luckily, we were only
given a warning. A "next time" would mean our prompt affilia-
tion with the short list of Westbury's ex-students. Yet these types
of actions re-certified the bond between Paul and me. We were
so impressed with the life and example of Don Pedro—the
greatest modern-time nationalist—that Felipe, Paul, Juan and
me, called ourselves "La Sociedad de Albizu Campos."

Mutin came to Old Westbury a few weekends in late November and I introduced her as "my fiancée." Just before leaving for
Old Westbury in the fall of 1968 we decided to have a big party
at Arnie's Chez José, where I presented her with an engagement

ring. We didn't set a date, but we knew we would get married sometime in the near future.

We returned to school after Christmas and intersession without an inkling of the impact 1969 would have on all of our lives. As part of my work-study program I was assigned to the admissions department to recruit Latino students. The college was dedicated to increasing the minority-student representation on campus. On a cold Tuesday in February, Pat Sweeney and I climbed into her black Volkswagen and headed to Chicago where I was to recruit Latino students. Pat worked at the admissions office at Westbury and was originally from Chicago. Traveling through frigid temperatures and snowstorms in Ohio and Indiana, we finally arrived in the gray Windy City of the Midwest. Nonstop driving had got us to Pat's hometown in a little under twenty-four hours. The whole trip was a blur. All I remembered was the white lines of the road passing at sixty and seventy miles per hour as I drove and looked over my left shoulder onto the road. When we arrived I slept for fourteen hours.

The next day we set out to follow our leads. We drove to the Loop and I saw Lake Michigan frozen. Knowing her way around the snow-filled city, Pat would drop me off and pick me up from my meetings with various Latino (Mexican/Puerto Rican) organizations. In addition to recruiting new students, we also interviewed prospective students who had applied to Old Westbury.

One day Pat dropped me off in front of the offices of the Latin American Defense Organization (LADO) to see my contact there, Obed Lopez. I walked up a long flight of stairs to the front desk and announced myself, stating I had an appointment. Obed came out and signaled me to his office. I told him all about

Old Westbury and its mission to attract socially and politically conscious students. We also talked politics. We both needed to make sure we agreed on the fundamentals of social justice and independence. I further explained that life experience and field study were integral parts of the overall curriculum for students entering Old Westbury, the College of Politics, Economics, and Society in particular. He began to get excited about this innovative concept in higher education.

I asked him if he knew any high-school students who were willing to go away to attend college in New York. He mentioned someone who was active in the community, and went to get him. I waited for about half an hour and Obed returned with a light-skinned young man, about my age, with reddish blond hair underneath a purple beret. This was Cha-Cha Jimenez from the Young Lords. He could have said, "This is Mambo Rodriguez from the Old Saints"—I had no idea who I had just met. It just didn't click. I sat with Cha-Cha and repeated the Old Westbury spiele. He said he knew a high-school student that was involved in a student struggle to rename their school "Roberto Clemente High School," who might be interested. Before he left, Cha-Cha said he would be back shortly after three.

I waited around, and at three p.m., Cha-Cha came back: "This is the high-school student I was talking to you about . . . David Pérez." David and I sat for a long time and talked about the war in Vietnam, the national black movement, his future education, and Puerto Rico. He was very much aware of police brutality in our barrios and all the community issues confronting the Latino people of Chicago. He also spoke proudly to me about the guy in the purple beret and his political gang, the Young Lords Organization (YLO). I told him about Juan, Felipe, and Paul, and about our struggles to uncover our history as Puerto Ricans. Within a couple of hours David and I had become fast friends.

I sat at his side while he filled out the Old Westbury application right there so that I could submit it at once. Before I left Chicago, I went back to thank Cha-Cha with a newfound respect. I knew that we would be connected in the future and that I would meet up with David in June at Old Westbury.

The day before I left Chicago I got a call from Charlie Young, who had accompanied Mutin to get her pregnancy-test results. He said, "Papo, you're going to be a papa." The drive back to New York seemed an eternity. I couldn't get back fast enough. Mutin and I had to figure out our lives immediately. We got married in early March and lived on campus in a two-room apartment.

Paul had gone to Mexico for a Spanish-culture immersion and to learn the language of our people. I had stayed in touch with Felipe and Juan while he was gone. Upon his return, Paul was no longer Paul. Now he was Pablo. Not only did he become Pablo, he became Pablo "Yoruba" Guzmán—a complete transformation. That time had the power of altering hundreds of thousands of us in search of our identity, our true history and pride within ourselves.

La Sociedad was now complete with Yoruba's return, and we resumed our meeting at the RGS offices. We kept a close watch on the hundreds of student takeovers all over the country, the merger of the SNCC (Student Nonviolent Coordinating Committee) with the Black Panther Party (BPP) and the formation of the Rainbow Coalition under the leadership of Chicago BPP state chairman Fred Hampton. The Rainbow Coalition was an interesting development for us in New York. The Coalition was made up of the BPP, YLO, American Indian Movement (AIM), and the Young Patriots—an all-poor-white organization with roots in the Appalachian Mountains.

Our frustrations begged for a change from a study group to

organization-building. We saw other national minorities raising their voices and taking to the streets, and not a word from the Puerto Ricans in the Northeast. When David arrived and joined La Sociedad, we began to move rapidly toward abandoning college and campus life and returning to our community. Yoruba, David, Denise, Roberto, and Marelene Cintrón left school.

We were all between nineteen to twenty-one years old. David told us the story of the Young Lords (the gang) and its transformation into a political organization. In June we had decided to go to Chicago to request official authorization to become the East Coast chapter of the YLO. Since David knew Cha-Cha and I had recently met him, we set up the meeting with the national office. I proceeded to get back on the road to Chicago, this time not to recruit Latinos for a college, but to commit to a revolution. Upon our request they told us that they had recently approved another small group in El Barrio. Cha-Cha suggested that when we got back to New York, we should merge with the other group. It was a formality. After only one day of talks, we agreed, and returned from Chicago as Young Lords. Later, establishing contact with the Barrio Lords to arrange the merger was relatively easy, as we knew every socially active youth in the area. One of their leaders was a photographer named, Juan "Fi" Ortiz. He was younger than all of us, but negotiations went well and the merger of both groups was accomplished in one day. Now Fi had become a member of the YLO Central Committee.

Meanwhile, other major events were taking shape. Preparations were being made for a rock festival to be held in upstate New York by mid-August. The Woodstock Music and Arts Fair had been planned as a gathering for some fifty thousand fans, but was attracting no attention at all from the mainstream media. At the end, more than half a million people gathered at the festival, which created the unexpected fantasy of a virtual "nation" that lasted three days and was completely devoted to music, peace, marijuana and love. Jimi Hendrix, Janis Joplin, the Who, and Santana were among the many performers that gave that rock festival something more than content—soul. The media had failed by overlooking the phenomenon. That was easy, since the real story had to do more with the way in which the youth rebellion was spreading across the country. Easy explanations are destined to fail in any assessment of 1969. Looking back, however, clear footprints appear. During that summer, young men and women from different ethnic backgrounds, all with a sense of disenfranchisement and repulsed by oppression, were trying to put together a coalition with a simple goal: We just wanted to reach the unreachable star, and dream the impossible—that is, to fulfill the promise of "justice for all" in America.

The time had arrived to make the official and public announcement that the YLO had a chapter in New York. We had become part of an organization that had a philosophical likeness to groups like the Youth Against War and Fascism (YAWF), all the Socialist Party affiliates, the Communist Party USA, the Youth International Party (Yippies), La Casa de Las Americas, Movimento Pro-Independencia (MPI). We participated in our first public demonstration in Tompkins Square Park in the East Village, commemorating the sixteenth anniversary of the attack on Moncada, Cuba by Fidel Castro, and the tenth anniversary of the Cuban Revolution, on Saturday, July 26, 1969. Felipe took the microphone and announced that the Young Lords were in New York "to serve and protect the best interests of the Puerto Rican community." Without an office, platform, or program, we went back to El Barrio to start the revolution.

NOBODY LIKES GARBAGE

BY THE SUMMER OF 1969 Felipe Luciano, Pablo "Yoruba" Guzmán, Juan González, Juan "Fi" Ortiz, David Pérez, and I were always aware that our young lives were on the line: The price for revolution could easily include death or prison. Still, we all made up our minds to step forward.

Why?

It was a world of revolution and we did not want to be left out.

Barely a year before, in 1968, a radical movement had overwhelmed the streets of France. Reports from Paris told the world how the capital of France was engulfed in flames, barricaded, with students exchanging stones for bullets with the police. In the middle of the riot, someone had written on a street wall a slogan that summarized the historical agenda that millions of young people had begun to embrace around the planet: "WE SHALL BE REALISTIC, LET'S DO THE IMPOSSIBLE."

The student revolt in Paris sparked uprisings throughout France and inspired uprisings in many other countries, including the United States. Within days, the movement had engulfed the University of Paris, La Sorbonne, and had been joined by workers all around France, which seized up many factories, prompting the end of French president Charles de Gaulle's mandate in 1969. The French leader resigned after a majority of voters rejected his proposals for a referendum on constitutional reforms. The reverberations of France's uprisings, "Paris 1968," heavily impacted the radical student movement in the United States.

It was also the era of third-world liberation struggles. Africa was transforming itself from being an area almost completely subject to European colonial rule, to a continent replete with independent nations. Between 1951 and 1975, forty-six African colonies declared nationhood and independence from their colonizers—nations which remain autonomous today. Independent black Africa was not just existing, it was thriving, becoming a launching pad for literature, the arts, politics, and above all, genuine cultural pride. The CIA-sponsored murders of nationalist giants like Patrice Lumumba of the Congo in 1961 did nothing to keep Africa from rising. A Muslim revival was also beginning to take shape in the region.

In Latin America, the year 1968 saw a military coup seize power in Peru, taking control of foreign business companies, saying they were sneaky powerbrokers in the almost five hundred thousand–square–mile country with a variety of land, climate, customs, and two great cultures, Indian and Spanish, living side by side. At the same time, Omar Torrijos had started to overthrow the elitist government in Panama, and promised to establish a popular democracy and to recover the Panama canal, at the time a colonial possession of the United States. Guerrilla movements like the Montoneros in Argentina, the Tupacamaros in Uruguay, the Sandinistas in Nicaragua, and the many other insurrectionary movements in Latin America served as encouragement for us to take action back home.

Events just south of the border, in Mexico, were also provoking outrage. In the labyrinth of Tlatelolco Square in Mexico City, the police had surrounded and killed hundreds of students demonstrating against the social conditions in their country. The massacre took place right beside an old colonial church where there's a statue depicting Juan Diego, the Indian who had the vision of making the Virgin Mary a magnificent symbol of Mexican Independence.

That same year—1968—the Catholic bishops in Latin America met in Medellín, Colombia, in a show of the church's support for the struggle for human rights and social improvements taking place in Colombia. The Medellín conference provided the atmosphere for the growth of many radical grassroots movements on the continent. The theology of liberation gave church approval for social and economic change—very important in these devout Catholic countries.

As the Vietnam War raged in Southeast Asia, the Tet Offensive exacted a heavy toll on American soldiers. The My Lai Massacre only added gasoline to the fire of outrage surrounding our military presence in Vietnam. Images broadcast all over the world on the evening news became symbols of the United States' acts of inhumanity against a very poor nation.

The United States was determined to travel far to stop independent rule. Vietnam refused to become an economic colony.

It would not allow "private capitalist enterprises" subsidized by the United States government to invest in their country. The United States wanted to demonstrate to the world its resolve, covertly and in open armed confrontation, to stop any national liberation movement. Ernesto "Che" Guevara led the call to attack U.S. imperialism with "many Vietnams" all around Latin America, a signal for all nations to rise to their own revolutions. Today, the failure to understand what Guevara meant led a few Washington politicians, from the president down, to wrongfully believe that since the Soviet Union was no longer willing to back the Cuban revolution, Castro's Cuba had become easy prey. The Cuban revolution, as well as anti-imperialist sentiment in Latin America, Africa, and even Europe, had its roots in the history of those nations that have struggled against U.S. or European colonization. It didn't rest on foreign aid.

The United States was not exempt from the radical trend, but it certainly was a reluctant debutante. The mid-1960s witnessed the development of a strong and diverse African-American civil-rights movement in the U.S., only to be dealt a severe blow by the assassination of Dr. Martin Luther King, Jr. in Memphis, Tennessee, in 1968. By the second half of the decade, the feminist movement was awakening with great strength, particularly among women of color. The American Indian Movement (AIM) was gaining force. It was during that year also that the gay community in New York, tired of harassment, met with force a police raid at the Stonewall Inn in a fight that lasted for two full days and marked the origin of the contemporary gay pride movement.

The National Democratic Convention in Chicago in 1968 became the meeting point for many grassroots groups who went there with their own grievances, just to be met by a brutal police force that chased and clubbed demonstrators at will, as the victims chanted: "The whole world is watching! The whole world is watching!"

Chegüí always told the story about his time in Chicago with his friend, author Norman Mailer. They had gone together to cover the 1968 National Democratic Convention for a magazine. They shared a large room with two king-size beds at a hotel in the center of town. One night, around nine-thirty P.M., they walked together through the troubled streets near the Convention Center and, as Chegüí was accustomed to, a few National Guardsmen recognized him and one sergeant started to introduce him to each and every one of his colleagues, about fifteen in all. He chatted and signed autographs for some time.

Once they got back to the room, Norman decided to go out again, twenty to thirty minutes later.

"I don't need you for now," he told Chegüí. "In fact, you should rest for a while. I'll see you in an hour or so." Norman smiled to himself. "But please, do not step out of this room unless you talk to me first."

Chegüí nodded in approval and as Norman slammed the door, he put the TV on and went to bed. A few minutes later he was fast asleep.

Two to three hours later, he was awakened by a bad dream, and, automatically, stared at the TV. A minute later he saw his close friend Norman being taken to jail in handcuffs. Chegüí jumped off the bed in shock, picked up the phone, and called his wife, Ramona, in New York. As he spoke with her regarding the arrest of his friend, the hotel operator interrupted the call, saying that Mr. Torres had an important call coming in.

It was Norman. "I'm out of jail," he yelled. "Please, stay there. Don't you move from the room!"

History would record the bloody incidents in Chicago as a

"police riot." Uniformed National Guardsmen and local and state police, had decided that Norman, as well as many other sympathizers and organizers of the young protesters—all of them United States citizens—were the guilty ones, opening the door for the supersensational trial of the Chicago Seven.

During that period, Bob Dylan said it best, when he sang: *"You don't need a weatherman to know which way the wind blows."*

Now it was our turn.

We believed the working class should have a greater voice in shaping society. It was as simple as that. We saw "the State" as a repressive tool, which only protected the wealthy and was incapable of being fair or legitimate to the people. That meant the millions of American workers who earned their living by selling their labor should be liberated from having to carry on their shoulders the few rich ones. For us, the problem was even worse. We felt that Puerto Rican workers were not only deprived of the riches resulting from their work, but also from the basic human right of having their own nation. The news coming from Puerto Rico encouraged us. The independence movement was gaining strength, and students at the University of Puerto Rico were staging violent protests against the military presence. The Young Lords were not just a group of barrio boys yearning for adventure and recognition. We aspired to help develop a world we desperately wanted to be a part of. We had a cause and now was the time.

First we decided to educate ourselves. We read books on how Mao Tse-tung had unleashed the revolutionary forces in China, and on Ho Chi Minh's strategies to liberate Vietnam—anything we thought would help us. Toiling at our studies, we developed a good sense of what the people needed and how to proceed in order to succeed in political struggles . . . or so we thought.

The time came when we felt prepared to discuss and debate the true needs of the poor with the relevant people of our society: the media, intellectuals and politicians, and, most important, the Puerto Rican people. Such a task was easier said than done. Our barrage of sophisticated philosophical ideas and revolutionary readings served us no good when discussing the approach with the common people of our barrios.

"We must go to them . . . to the masses," said Juan. "They may know something we don't. So, first we must go to the people of El Barrio."

Even now, as I recall that conversation, I feel the intensity of that moment. We were full of romantic ideas and confident of having a strong hold on the truth. We all decided to go to the streets the next weekend and talk to the people.

On Saturday morning, I dressed in the usual youth uniform of those days: jeans, Converse sneakers, and a T-shirt. It was several weeks before the Lords would adopt the revolutionary dress code of U.S. Army–issued field jackets, combat boots, and purple berets with a YLO button. While I was driving from Long Island to Manhattan in my old '63 Volkswagen, I didn't give too much thought to the revolutionary task ahead. I was preoccupied with my wife who was pregnant. We were both worried about our new responsibility. However, once we got started, those thoughts did not prevent me from getting completely emotionally involved in our first political action.

The streets were filled with the strong fragrance of *alcapurria* and *bacalaítos fritos*, the sounds of Tito Puente, Machito, Eddie Palmieri, and El Gran Combo blaring out of every storefront and open window. This was our barrio, where it was safe to express our culture, far away from the eyes and ears of those who had no understanding of our complex rhythmical patterns. Here we could be ourselves.

Near the Lexington Avenue subway station, at the corner of 110th Street, there was a social club with men, mostly middle-aged, dressed in T-shirts and dungarees, with cans of *la fría* (cold beer) resting at their ankles, playing dominoes and listening to the jukebox. We decided to approach them first.

That simple action, of course, was not that simple. We all went over to them together. So there we were, a group of six Nuyorican (except for David) youngsters with an embarrassingly limited knowledge of Spanish, trying to have a fluent and meaningful conversation with men of another generation whose main language was precisely Cervantes'. With the memory of the riots that had erupted the year before on these same streets, we were now asking the people what they thought should be the first thing to be changed in their community.

"Just take a look. See by yourselves," said one of the men playing dominoes. "Don't you see the garbage all throughout the streets? It is overflowing the entire area with smelly odor . . . everywhere! Don't you smell it? It's horrible!" He was sitting with his back to the wall, his olive-tanned skin adorned with tattoos. He spoke in Spanish and accented English. But he didn't bother to grant us all his attention. He spoke while his eyes and hands were glued to the game.

One of them pointed to the messy street, others to the cans that emerged from the piles of garbage.

"What did he say?" I asked, after we were safely away from the domino players. We looked at each other in disbelief. It was not quite what we were looking for. After all, Marx, Lenin, Mao, Che, Albizu, Uncle Ho, Cabral—none of them ever spoke of garbage. But they all did, nevertheless, speak about "the legitimate needs and aspirations of the people."

The idea of garbage was surprising enough, but I think we were all also a little surprised that no one in El Barrio seemed to know that just a few weeks before, we had announced the establishment of a branch of the Young Lords in New York. We were simply not recognized. *Uprising* and *revolution*, or even *socialism*, were not words included in the people's vocabularies, and they could have cared less about those terms.

Had we approached the correct people? Or were they alienated from their own reality as a by-product of the effect of their political oppression and colonial mentality?

We thought of the possibility of having used the wrong approach. In our minds we saw that if we expressed clear options, the "masses" would select the more worthy causes.

So we walked toward a building where women were walking out with shopping carts en route to *la marqueta*. Some were older ladies, the sort we respectfully and affectionately call *doñas*. This time we were more cautious. David, who was the more fluent in Spanish since he was born and had spent his childhood in Lares, a strongly nationalist mountain town in the center of Puerto Rico, did the talking. He asked them the same question about changes in the community. He went further, in an effort to refresh their collective memories, mentioning issues like housing, police brutality, crime, and poverty.

"Look at the garbage!" said one of the *doñas*. "It smells! For how long do we have to take this?"

The vehemence of their outrage was surprising to us only because we failed to recognize the obvious.

We then went slowly from 112th through 115th Streets down Third Avenue. And there were more conversations. The reply was overwhelmingly the same. As the afternoon progressed, we began to slowly accommodate ourselves to the concern of the people. After that, whenever we approached them we would start a conversation including the garbage problem. It was amazing, as if they had discussed the garbage issue among themselves for weeks. Their responses were practically identical everywhere. We talked to workingmen and -women of all ages, to the youth and to people in the neighborhood who were just hanging out.

That Saturday we ended up in a small apartment of a friend in El Barrio, where the bathtub sat in the kitchen. At once we started to unpack the cooked rice and pink beans we had bought in a nearby restaurant. As we enjoyed the meal, we talked about what had happened.

I was more than just surprised. I think the others felt the same way. The truth was that the masses we intended to help had treated us like a bunch of ignorant punks, asking us to open our eyes to the obvious. In our collective imagination we just wanted them to verify our ideas of their problems, but they didn't. It was our first humbling experience. We not only listened, we heard our people.

Juan spoke first. "What is it?" he asked.

"Garbage," a voice answered.

"Garbage," a second voice said.

I said, "Garbage!"

There were some laughs, of the type usually shrouding shame. Some tried in vain to hide their smiling faces, while others lost control and began to laugh at full volume.

"If they said garbage," Juan said seriously, his eyes searching for ideas in his head, "then that's it: Garbage!"

It was getting late and my mind was no longer focused on the discussion. Soon thereafter, I started to go back to Long Island, as my head entertained images of my eight-month-pregnant wife and our first child, soon to be born. Of course, during the long ride back to the Old Westbury campus, thoughts about El Barrio and "the garbage" bounced back and forth against the walls of my mind.

That Saturday we had discovered a simple truth about the

needs of our community. We concluded that sometimes truth is a matter of perspective, of being able to see through the eyes of others.

Right then and there I realized knowledge comes from experience rather than study. Both are valuable, but so different from each other. One of the problems that seem to afflict people in power is that the nature of their status prohibits them from understanding the experiences of common people. The elite simply can't submit themselves to the day-to-day difficulties faced by the masses of people. Consequently, they lack the opportunity to learn about relevant problems of the larger society. They lack the ability to develop a human and spiritual connection based on the economic and political realities of others. It's something that cannot be learned from a book or a theory.

That's the paradox of our own desires, the damaging poverty hidden in wealth. Often we strive for a fortune that would liberate us from want, from the shortcomings of scarcity and dependence on others. But on many occasions, success brings along a new form of deprivation. The powerful, the rich, and the famous tend to live in a world inhabited by the few, surrounded by conditions not shared by the many. Too often their knowledge about the real life of the majority of the people is limited to experience acquired during the few instances in which they venture into poor neighborhoods. They simply overlook the diverse and rich spectrum of poor people's experience.

Something quite similar happens with theoretical and academic knowledge.

Although I can trace our own commitment back to our childhoods and the needs of our people, our revolutionary ideas and conceptions came first from books. Also, despite our particular experience as poor but privileged due to our college education, somehow we had distanced ourselves from our own broader identity.

Here was still another important limitation to our ability to read beforehand from the open book of the neighborhood. We had been absent from our communities for many years and were now just returning for good.

The world was changing so fast that it seemed almost impossible for the common person to keep pace. Starting in the late 1950s, when the Soviets put the first satellite in space, the first dog in space, and the first man in space, America pushed hard and in 1969, just a few weeks before we set our revolutionary feet in El Barrio, U.S. astronauts stepped on the moon.

Our world was full of miniskirts, Afro haircuts, the Age of Aquarius, space exploration, rock, salsa, ethnic awakening, and revolution.

We saw ourselves as teachers for the alienated masses. By thinking that we knew all that was worth knowing, and believing that by reading a couple of books about the revolution we could easily become revolutionary leaders, showed our inexperience, not real street smartness.

We needed a cure from our many learning handicaps if we were to succeed, and our own people were providing us with a remedy.

The people of El Barrio taught us to open our eyes to the experience of the people. After the shocking fact-finding mission around the streets of El Barrio, it became clear why garbage was such an important issue. As a community we were denied the resources of municipal government. Sanitation trucks drove through our community to get to the more "affluent" pockets of the city. In the middle- and upper-class white neighborhoods of the Bronx, Queens, and Brooklyn, away from this Latino community, garbage was not spread in the streets and on the sidewalks. The people in those neighborhoods did not have to spend their mornings or evenings cleaning their sidewalks. The New York City Department of Sanitation did it for them. The smell of rotten food and the stockpiles of garbage were left untouched in El Barrio for long days, right in front of building entrances, playgrounds, and schools.

For the chic, upper-class breed, clean areas are more associated with the aesthetics of the community. For poor people, garbage and filth are more related to poor health conditions and injustice.

How much did we really understand of that lesson? I can't tell, since I'm still learning from it today. At least, after that dialogue with the people, we not only had a cause and a purpose, we also had a solid starting point. Now we needed an office. All political parties have one, don't they?

While strolling in the neighborhood that Saturday, we had spotted a number of vacant storefronts on 111th Street, between Second and Third Avenues. The one we selected was a small square space with a front glass window. A week later, it was to become the official headquarters of the Young Lords Organization in New York. Of course, in order to turn it into an office, we had to find chairs, tables, and equipment. Besides, the place had to be cleaned and painted. Local people and community organizations donated used office equipment and paint.

We were in the process of analyzing, with the typical academic/socialistic mind, the lessons to be learned from our conversations with the neighbors, but we were also putting our office in working order. Many discussions took place while we swept the floor of our brand-new headquarters.

After organizing the office, the logical step was to clean the sidewalk in front, and then clean the whole block. Indeed, we never lacked volunteers. They came with their own brooms, or asked us to assign them one. In that simple unplanned fashion, the first Young Lords offensive began to take form.

The process was certainly not self-propelled at all. We were having extensive meetings. Looking back, perhaps we talked too much. We were all radicals from college. In those endless sessions, Juan was always the theoretician delineating lessons from our past. Felipe was more an action guy, and David, our wise *jibarito*, reflected more on how people would react to our ideas or actions. I played the role of mediator. After all, I had brought all these people together and they allowed me that position of honor within the group. I heard all the opinions and put together what appeared to be a consensus.

It was during one of those sessions that Juan González came up with the name "the Garbage Offensive." We'd probably learned it from the Vietnam War. For the Vietnamese, every programmed political or military action was labeled an "offensive." The more we spoke and extended the plan to clean up our barrio, the more enthusiastic we became. We finally concluded that this was the people's request. If we did a good job, it would open a huge door of confidence between the community of El Barrio and the Young Lords.

We were ready to take action. Yoruba, our minister of information, would notify the media. As our physical and mental energy gained momentum, ideas started to flow. As in a work-study program, we had been cleaning the streets the best we could with our house brooms. After a week or so of doing this, we came to realize that we were doing the work of the Department of Sanitation. So why not demand some help from that agency?

One bright sunny Sunday morning we decided to visit the

Department of Sanitation and ask for some large brooms. A bunch of Lords and a few community volunteers went to a local office of the agency. Felipe faced the man at the Sanitation office. He was tall, well built, and firm. Unaffected, Felipe went straight to the point.

"Can we have a few brooms to clean up our dirty streets in El Barrio?" Felipe was staring assertively at the man across the counter.

Confused, the city official didn't know what to make of such a request.

"We can't do that," the large man guarding the place said. "We have to follow orders and regulations."

"Is that your final decision?" Felipe asked coolly.

"That's it, young man," the man responded.

"Now, you mean final—not a chance for us to get a few of our brushes to clean the streets of our barrio?"

The big man nodded with confidence, denying our request.

It took just a few seconds. After pushing the strong man to the side, Felipe put both hands over the counter and jumped over, inviting his companions, more than ten men and women, to do the same. In less than a minute they had misappropriated ten large brooms. Without looking back, they walked out. Half an hour later we were at the Young Lords' headquarters making plans for what to do next.

Now armed with large brooms, the Lords and some volunteers swept the street and stockpiled large quantities of garbage.

The only problem was that the trucks of the Department of Sanitation did not come. When at last they did, half the garbage was left scattered all over the area. It was a slap in the face. This had to stop. At that moment we decided to take the struggle to another level.

The following Sunday would change our lives forever. That

morning when I kissed my wife good-bye, I told her nothing about where I was going or what the Lords intended to do, but she knew that we were up to something. I left home at eight-thirty in the morning, and drove to El Barrio. I did not regret not telling her about the details because it was not my intention to worry her. Our baby was due in September and I did not want to complicate things. I did worry. Actually, I was scared. My thinking was that it would be an important day, but there was no way to foresee how important. Someone could get hurt or arrested.

My mouth was cotton-dry. What we were about to do could end in a confrontation with the police. Besides the physical pain, a clash with the law might imply a military defeat. Yet no one was willing to give up. We'd developed a sense of courage and determination.

Engaged in those thoughts, I arrived at the area where I was supposed to leave my car. For security reasons we had decided to park our cars far away from the office in El Barrio, which forced us to walk ten to fifteen blocks to work every single day.

I got to the office an hour and a half later, after finding a secure spot for my car. Two or three of the members were already on the sidewalk in front of the building. We entered the office, where we had already decorated the walls with posters of our heroes: Pedro Albizu Campos, the Black Panthers, Ho Chi Minh, Che Guevara. The brooms taken from the Department of Sanitation, cans of lighter fluid, and matches were waiting for us in the office.

That Sunday morning, in the company of over thirty adult volunteers, we started to sweep the garbage into the streets, particularly around bus stops and the center of Second and Third Avenues, near 106th, 111th, 116th, and 118th Streets.

There were the young and the old joining us. I can remember

a middle-aged woman in a house robe. She was short, with heavy eyeglasses. She just kept sweeping until her working area was thoroughly clean. People from the surrounding blocks came; the numbers of people began to multiply rapidly.

I will never forget another woman, a very heavyset woman with a long dress, sweeping the sidewalk in front of her building on the south side of 112th Street between Second and Third Avenues. She was dancing and laughing. Yet beneath those actions I perceived fear in her. It was an apprehension I noticed not only among the adult volunteers rallying with us, but also in some of our own members.

In an instant, though, I recognized that such feelings were not due to the possibility of being arrested, hurt, or even killed, but because of the likelihood of defeat. After all, we were expecting to face one of the strongest and most sophisticated police forces in the country. Again, to lose to them was to fail the masses. It would be a crippling blow.

While pushing garbage into the street, I saw the man who just a few weeks before had been playing dominoes in front of the social club on 110th Street, the one who had surprised us by stating that the big issue was garbage. He was watching from a distance in silence. There was also the woman from the nearby building who had pointed out the garbage problem during our first, eye-opening expedition.

All day we were very busy accumulating the garbage. This move was intended to announce the imminence of serious trouble waiting ahead. The garbage formed a five-foot-high wall across the six lanes of Third Avenue, causing an unexpected traffic jam. Some drivers cursed and screamed at the piles of garbage and at us. Others nodded their heads and blew the horns of their cars in admiration of this never-before-seen strategy in ghetto politics. The only choice we had was confrontational politics.

Yoruba, with juvenile enthusiasm and soaked with sweat, raised his voice, and screamed: "Let's burn it! Burn the garbage!"

Immediately, our minister of education, Juan González, took a bullhorn and started to direct the already jammed traffic away from the pile. The torching of the accrued garbage was about to take place. More people left their apartments and joined the growing crowd while we proceeded to spread the lighter fluid. I did not count the people but in my recollection, there could have been five hundred or five thousand neighbors taking part in this garbage protest. Every single Young Lord threw a match. Every single person of our community who had helped, threw matches. In a matter of minutes it was like an ancient ceremony, with flames aiming high into the skies, reaching to touch our gods. It was a collective cry of "*¡Basta ya!*"—"Enough!"

As the garbage burned and the flames grew, people nearby cheered spontaneously. We all felt the spirit of winning, the triumph of good over evil, where justice, in this moment, prevailed. I remembered the revolutionary and spiritual marriage with the people. The dominoes players, the *doñas*, and the Young Lords had all found themselves in the middle of the garbage protest. At that moment we knew we were victorious.

Indeed it was a theatrical scene. Flames went up spectacularly as people started to scream with joy. In my mind the people—timid mothers, grandmothers, everyone—were showing the world their support for the Young Lords' action. This new sight brought to mind the riots of 1967 . . . but this time the protest was flawlessly organized.

Of course, the police were already on the scene. On that Sunday the spirit of the people, the righteousness of the demand, and the role of the Young Lords, held the police immobilized.

None of us were arrested. We all got away. The ones who acted were the journalists; on a typical news-dead summer Sunday, we became the lead story.

When I got home, tired but proud, the story had already hit the TV newscasts. My wife was justifiably concerned. While I tried to keep my revolutionary ego focused on watching the news, she was quarreling. How come I was devoting my efforts on that garbage issue instead of preparing for our child to come? I think I answered her back with some revolutionary rhetoric and disregarded her concerns. I realize now it was an immature response. There is no easy victory on the road to real revolution for social justice. Part of that road reveals how we should treat each other and how connected we become to those we care for and love. I hadn't walked that path yet. The ability to strike a balance between a political and military victory and preparing for my child eluded me at the time. I am not sure I could have done it differently.

Nonetheless, the Garbage Offensive was a rousing success and a revelation. For people growing up in a culture with respect for authority, such political action was a categorical breakthrough for Puerto Ricans in the United States. The colonial pathology of docility had been overcome through successful collective action. The dormant Puerto Rican community in the United States was waking up.

The story reached City Hall in New York, and Mayor Lindsay became very concerned. He had good cause to worry. He didn't want to deal with new riots in El Barrio, and now had several reasons to pay attention to what was going on there.

One was his campaign as a candidate for a second term in office, something that was proving more difficult than anticipated. As a matter of fact, many analysts had predicted that he would not run again. His liberal politics had been regarded as a failure for the city. On top of that, his administration had been afflicted by severe cash shortages, unrest, inadequate services, strikes in public services, and a middle-class portion of New Yorkers were dissatisfied with him, claiming that the mayor had an unwarranted preference toward poor neighborhoods at the expense of taxpayers.

Lindsay was one of a kind. Instead of denying the claims against him with a typical media campaign, he positioned himself as the candidate who accepted his shortcomings. He did not retreat from his commitments. On the contrary, he tried his best to assure the people that he was not only ready to take the blame but to continue pushing as hard as possible toward some sort of more humane government.

There was also another element in his attempt to continue in office. The previous year, the right-wing Richard M. Nixon, had won the United States presidency. Options for the city if Lindsay were defeated were worsened dramatically.

A few days after the garbage was burned, Arnaldo Segarra, now a special assistant to Mayor Lindsay, visited his old neighborhood. Arnie and I knew each other well from the organizing we had done together during the summer after the 1967 riots. He reached out to me and explained that he wanted to find out what was going on uptown. He was very straightforward—the mayor could not afford to let this issue get out of hand.

I introduced Arnie to the Central Committee of the Young Lords.

We couldn't believe it. How had we gotten the mayor of New York City to want to negotiate with us?

"There is no negotiation with us. Go to the street and talk to the people," Felipe answered.

Such a demand was not a threat to a guy like Arnie. Besides the fact that he'd always been an honest man, he was also from

those barrio streets. He just went outside with us. Before beginning our tour, we had the very familiar and simple ceremony of
gulping a *piragüa* on the street corner.

Many years later, during a conversation with a journalist, Arnie was to remember that day. He had not forgotten the *piragüa*,
and even said what syrup it had: coconut. Well, he was that kind
of official, the type who had developed a sensitive sense for politics and opportunity, was savvy on the details, a master of figuring people out. He also had the practicality to pay attention
to us in El Barrio. He knew that regardless of his opinions about
our radical politics, the only chance his boss had was to navigate
the stream of upheavals in the poor neighborhoods.

Back then, the city simply lacked the resources to cover all
areas with their outdated sanitation trucks. Moreover, by influencing the communities that were organizing themselves, Lindsay could somehow claim that process as a political victory for
himself. That way, he would appear to be delivering something—
a government with ears for the people. A government of some
350,000 civil servants, most of them drowning in a sea of red
tape and paperwork, was not a useful machine to convey the
image that someone was listening to the people's many daily
grievances. But by using a strategy of reaching out with highly
capable guys like Arnie, and by taking advantage of groups like
ours, Lindsay was able to create the perception that someone
was willing to go the extra mile to do something about the problem. With people enduring long-lasting problems, to have a government that went along with them in petitioning a redress of
grievances prevents many from pointing the finger too harshly.

Whether Arnie shared this perception of reformist politics or
not, I don't know. We had good reasons, too, for going along
with this approach, and even forcing the hand in that direction.
We were revolutionaries. An "offensive" has no value in itself; it

is a political tool. It is a resource in the political education of the masses. What we intended to do was to show the people a path toward a high level of political consciousness, to understand the power that lies in the hands and the souls of the working people. Workers produce the wealth of the nation, and because of that, they shouldn't have to crawl and beg for charity from the government. The way to radical change begins with the people fighting for their rights. If you want clean streets, improvement of public health, or better housing, you have to struggle. In that sense, to discard reformists in government is a gross mistake for a revolutionary. Quite to the contrary, you have to support reformers in order to advance as much as possible the education of the masses. Of course, you will not stop there, because the goal is higher, but you go further only when conditions are right and the people are ready.

With our simple Garbage Offensive we had shown the people that we could be a very helpful force, and that they, too, could do something besides complaining. Strolling along with Arnie throughout the neighborhood without having to submit ourselves to the loyalty game of "political patronage first" was a paramount victory.

We walked along with Arnie and introduced him to the neighbors, telling them that he was the representative of the community in City Hall. Arnie listened to the people.

Arnie, as he has done for over thirty years as an insider in government, delivered. Shortly thereafter, the trucks of the Department of Sanitation began paying regular visits to El Barrio.

Now, after the Garbage Offensive, we trusted our people in El Barrio and they trusted us. They would now support and protect the Young Lords. There was also a practical lesson for all parties involved: When a community stands together and makes a strong statement, it will be heard. On this occasion, something had been done to address the problem. The same happened in all Young Lords offensives; it became our mantra: a balance of embarrassing the state, the city, and public and private institutions, and being able to present popular solutions to address the issue at hand.

People do not relate to defeat; but victory attracts support. Community groups and organizations began noticing us. Some of them were government-funded agencies and did not want to risk that support by getting directly involved. They would provide us with equipment, materials, and other subtle forms of support. At the same time, as they preferred to remain at a safe distance, we gained political space in which to maneuver.

That space, however, put us on the spot. By respectfully distancing themselves from us, the other groups had placed an added burden on our juvenile shoulders. We had acted differently and now we felt pressured to show that we actually were different. That part of our self-education process proved to be more difficult than expected. We did not always live up to our own high, idealistic expectations and standards. We wanted to incarnate the "new man and woman" of the revolution. The Italian political thinker Machiavelli once said that in politics, like in war, you aim with the bow higher than a straight line because that way, when the arrow makes its downward curve, it can still hit the target. The lesson is this: Do not be afraid of setting for yourselves the highest standards you can imagine for a better society. Go ahead and do it! Tense up the muscles of your bodies and your minds and try your best to live up to those standards. Just don't forget that failures and shortcomings are as human as triumphs and successes, and that part of any political education is to be humble enough to admit that it's a learning process.

We tried to set an example by our behavior. Sharing goods with each other as much as possible, we wanted to teach our society the way of solidarity, not egotism. We tried to force ourselves to the hard discipline that says that being poor does not imply indolence.

Not everyone understood that lesson.

I suspected that some of our friends saw some hints of hypocrisy in our attempts to change the way we were. Some of them believed that you should not advocate change unless you're changed yourself. I really thought it was the other way around. By trying to improve your behavior and your political awareness, even your limitations can assist in the education of the masses. That way you show the people that social change is made by people with real problems, trying their best to overcome oppression, not by being inaccessible heroes in ideal conditions.

With the help of the community we had learned about the importance of dealing with something as simple as garbage in order to organize a popular movement. In our quest to become true revolutionaries, we had learned to deal with our victory in the Garbage Offensive. For doing that, we received solid and effective community support. The people's awe-inspiring collaboration in the whole scheme of things was to become the single most important force behind the Young Lords' efforts. Although garbage collection in El Barrio improved, it never could be compared with the services that wealthier neighborhoods always enjoyed. Yet the experience helped us to understand the relationship between the political, the underground, the people, and the media that was needed to get our story told.

THE FIRST PEOPLE'S CHURCH

WE WERE ALL VERY EXCITED with the new and spectacular attention
the Garbage Offensive had generated for our efforts. We were
developing as an outstanding Puerto Rican organization, and
now, many more Puerto Ricans and other Latinos wanted to be
a part of the Young Lords. It was easy to get caught up in the
excitement. I noticed that our egos had to be reminded that our
priority was the betterment of our community. The organization
was only a way of making that happen, not an end in itself.

The Young Lords were about to join the people again and
stand up with pride even if it meant confrontation. And to stand
up—literally—was what we all did. It was a Sunday in December
1969, during the regular services at the First Spanish Methodist
Church of East Harlem. Some twenty Young Lords were among

the thirty or so parishioners attending the service. It was easy to spot members of the group. While the regular members of the congregation were wearing conservative civilian attire—some men with ties and the women with below-the-knee dresses—we were in full uniform: worn-out green military fatigue jackets and our trademark purple berets with our "TENGO PUERTO RICO EN MI CORAZÓN" ("PUERTO RICO IN MY HEART") buttons. We looked odd inside the recently remodeled redbrick church, but it was where we had decided to pick our fight.

To Reverend Humberto Carranza, a Cuban who went into exile in 1961 after being arrested three times by the revolutionary government of Fidel Castro, we must have looked like an all-too-familiar enemy with our beards and revolutionary rhetoric. In fact, we all wanted to look like, and emulate, Che. This time around, the reverend was in America and thought he could fight back. He had taken precautions and was ready to act. But so were we.

I had not been present at the Central Committee meeting that planned out the details for the Sunday testimonial. My wife and I had a lot of packing to do because that Sunday we were moving from Long Island to her father's house in Astoria, Queens. I had to move back to the city and be closer to the movement. Mutin also wanted to be closer to her family. Miguel Albizu, our son, was born on September 5, 1969, in Glen Cove Community Hospital in Long Island. I named him after my two heroes.

Felipe was to stand up during the testimonial period of the service and make a plea to the religious community to join the efforts of the Young Lords by providing space for social programs managed by us that we had already established in the community, including breakfast programs, clothing drives, and free public-health programs. It was a way to put pressure on Rever-

end Carranza, who had rejected our previous pleas to him. It was
the logical next step, after having made our proposal known to
the parishioners and the whole community through leaflets and
demonstrations in front of the church for weeks.

Busy moving, I heard what happened on the radio while driving into Queens with Mutin and Miguel Albizu. The newscaster
on CBS radio said that the police had prevented a takeover of
the First Spanish Methodist Church by the Young Lords. I knew
that at this point our intention was not to take over the church.
If it had been, the police would not have been able to prevent
it. I felt detached from my comrades who were in battle.

That night, after unloading our family belongings, I rushed
to El Barrio, but not before the already expected quarrel with
my wife. I told her she had known that something like this would
happen sooner or later; I had no choice but to go and help get
people out of jail.

When I reached the office, it was empty. Almost every member of the Central Committee was in jail. No one had the complete story. It didn't matter. I began making rounds of phone
calls to wealthy white liberals to raise the money for bail. I also
called the National Lawyer's Guild. I tried reaching Bob Blum,
Dick Ashe, Dan Myers, or a brilliant Latino lawyer, Jerry Rivers.
Jerry was the only Latino with the Guild and fought to represent
the Young Lords in all our legal cases. Jerry spent a lot of time
with us and soon enough, he went through a personal transformation much like Yoruba's after his trip to Mexico. One day he
came into the office and proudly announced that his name was
Geraldo Rivera. He was in court the next day at the bail hearing
for the Young Lords arrested at the church.

Finally, when all the members were back on regular duty, I
heard the whole story. Felipe was about to stand and proclaim

our demands to the congregation, only to be stopped by sudden turmoil. The police force was already there! As the police rushed inside the church, they spread throughout the hall, pushing people in every direction. Two of them approached Felipe with their billy clubs and ordered him to move. He stood firm even as the sticks were about to land on him. The whole attack lasted no more than a minute. But in that type of situation, sixty seconds feels like an eternity. Even choir members in robes participated in the police assault against us. When it was over, Felipe was bleeding profusely from a head wound that required eleven stitches. His left arm was also broken. Four more Young Lords were wounded, and thirteen arrested.

We all knew what we had to do next—seize the church. Such an action was consistent with the actions of the original Chicago Young Lords, who had staged a takeover a year earlier of a Methodist church and set up the Young Lords national office. We were going to follow their example.

The Methodist church had not distinguished itself in El Barrio for being progressive and community-focused. It was not in tune with what we perceived was one of the basic responsibilities of any church—to help people. East Harlem was a colorful but deprived community, where people from many Latino nationalities and races shared the same apartment walls. It was a mosaic of trades, from blue-collar workers to merchants. Above all, it was a neglected community. Many people there resided in dilapidated tenements, and in their day-to-day life had to cope with every conceivable scarcity. In summary, it was the kind of place for any religious institution to gain God's benediction by working overtime to help the neediest.

Under Reverend Carranza's guidance, the First Spanish Methodist Church of East Harlem was open only on Sundays for a worship service. Not a single social program was offered from that renovated building, which stood like an affront to the community groups looking for an appropriate location to provide direct services. We felt it was wrong. Our belief was that a church is a tax-exempt institution because it is supposed to serve the community spiritually and materially.

We saw Reverend Carranza as an enemy and maybe even a traitor to his own faith. He was a Cuban who was against the efforts of his own people to establish social justice and freedom from foreign intervention in their own land. From our point of view, he was just a *gusano* trying to prevent the revolution from taking place. Reverend Carranza's perspective was much different.

The influence of the church and its very presence in the Cuban political and social debate can be easily traced back to Father Varela, a Jesuit priest that protected the Catholic community in New York in the early nineteenth century and promoted the cultural and political awakening of Cuba. He was a strong promoter of Cuban interests and freedoms in Washington, during the times the Spanish ruled over the island. Cuban history regards him as the one who "taught the Cubans to think." So, after Father Varela, to say in Cuba that religion and politics do not mix is not only a mistake, it is a historical anachronism. During the revolutionary war of the 1950s, a book by another Jesuit, Father Freixedo, titled *Forty-eight Cases of Social Injustice*, was a strong denunciation of the oligarchic caste system that deprived the majority of Cubans of basic human dignity.

There was another church in Cuba as well. The efforts of illuminated social advocates in the church like Varela and Freixedo were counterbalanced by a system of priests and ministers who spread the notion of a religion that justified oppression. For them, God was an ever-watching omnipresent police presence to check your intimate sexual desires, but did not care if you starved to death. It was a God that considered it a sin to steal a pair of shoes, but gave benediction to the capitalists stealing the workers' salaries.

The communists' disdain for religion exacerbated the already hostile relationship between the masses and the church. With many priests and ministers preaching a faith devoid of social commitment to justice, and many communists being nonbelievers, the clash was inevitable. Carranza fled to the United States.

During the 1960s, the church became an important dynamo in the efforts to promote social justice in America. In the Deep South in particular, the church was a champion in the struggle to eliminate discrimination. In the Southwest, the church was present in the Mexican-American labor movement. We wanted that same responsiveness from the church for the Puerto Rican community in New York. I can understand Reverend Carranza's reluctance because of the image of his past that we represented. But we just wanted to establish a day-care center for the kids of working parents in our neighborhood and he was in our way.

By targeting the First Spanish Methodist Church we had two objectives: to challenge the institution to address the needs of its surrounding community, and to raise the consciousness of the people to take direct action as a method to resolve our collective needs. At the beginning, we wanted nothing more than for the church to provide us space during times not reserved for worship so we could conduct badly needed service programs. Now, with such force used to crush something as basic as the right to speak, we sensed that a takeover could be our only possible response.

We felt we had community support. Many local restaurants and grocery stores were willing to provide us with food for the breakfast programs. Yaya would always come back with enough food. Yaya was a Black Panamanian-American Korean War veteran with a plate in his head. He ran our breakfast programs, getting up at six in the morning five days a week to cook and then going out to get the kids into the program. Often we were greeted by a storeowner who refused to charge us because the merchandise was for "*los muchachos*," the kids. It was like having a "Barrio Card."

We had also developed a political position on the health-care system in the United States. We started going door-to-door to test children for lead poisoning. Juan González had learned that doctors at the Flower and Fifth Avenue Medical College suspected that certain health problems among the children of El Barrio could be caused by lead poisoning. The medical literature was available. The impact on humans by lead poisoning had been studied for decades. It was one thing to state this idea in theoretical terms, and quite another to live it. The problem was, the doctors only suspected lead poisoning—they lacked hard evidence. The matter was brought to the Central Committee.

Certain aspects of the proposed "Lead Offensive" were particularly important to us. It would strengthen our contacts with radical doctors in the hospital and the university. It would give us the opportunity to reveal a hidden enemy within the community. We would go the people and test the children. This would highlight our role as pro-active crusaders, as well as raising community awareness and consciousness. The garbage was something that could be seen easily by everyone. The cause-and-effect relationship was established simply by watching the rats and smelling the strong odor of the piles of waste. Microscopic lead poisoning was more deceptive. Here was a dangerous health situation that was invisible to the naked eye.

Although these were important considerations for the long-term goals of the YLO, none of them ever eclipsed our basic desire to improve living conditions within the community. Lead poisoning was a serious threat that provoked an immediate reaction from everyone in the YLO. There was a strong suspicion—almost a certainty—that the community was suffering a serious health hazard due to the negligence of the owners of many of the buildings in El Barrio. We decided that for every abusive landlord there should be a combative Young Lord. The Lead Offensive had begun.

Again, we began by canvassing the community—this time to test children for lead poisoning. Every Saturday morning for weeks, every member of the organization, regardless of rank, went into the projects and tenements of El Barrio to take blood samples. The results of the tests were shocking. The number of children who tested positive was staggering, the result of ingesting chips of the cheap lead-based paint landlords had used in these tenements for years. The long-term effects of lead in a child's body can be severe. Learning disabilities, decreased growth, hyperactivity, impaired hearing, and even brain damage can result from elevated lead levels.

The results of the tests were made public, and the crisis was addressed almost immediately due to the magnitude of the public health emergency we had revealed. Buildings throughout the five boroughs had been painted with the same cheap product. The number of children affected throughout the city was in the hundreds of thousands. In this case, Mayor Lindsay acted decisively and the use of lead-based paint was thereafter prohibited.

We were gaining recognition, and we were gaining members.

As soon as the Garbage Offensive had ended successfully, neighborhood youth had begun to come to our office and ask to join the Young Lords. In order to do so, they first had to learn about the richness of our Indio-African culture; the legacy of our history of resistance; and the history of national liberation struggles in Asia, Africa, and Latin America. Iris Morales and Juan designed a political education program. Three books formed the core of the program: Franz Fanon's *The Wretched of the Earth*, which addresses the psychological impact of colonialism and racism; *The Red Book* by Mao Tse-tung; and Che Guevara's *Man and Socialism: Transformation of the Individual*, which outlines the internal struggle of the individual to manifest change within himself in order to create a revolution in society. An aspirant to Young Lords membership was required to begin as a "friend of the Lords" (FOL), a phase in which he or she attended physical-education classes and mass mobilizations. Hiram Maristany photographed every FOL so that we could conduct background investigations to prevent infiltration from undercover agents. We had established a working relationship with two African-American organizations from the NYPD. These organizations had adopted resolutions not to infiltrate civil-rights or revolutionary movements, and were invaluable in helping us. I would go over every photo and identify potential infiltrators from the police department with each organization, and report back to the Central Committee. Many potential infiltrators had to find other assignments and yet others would be accepted and placed in the Ministry of Defense. That way, they could report back to their own superiors that they had been assigned to the Ministry, planning and coordinating direct actions, but they never actually planned a damn thing. We had them sell our newspaper *Pa'lante* ("Forward"). After passing the FOL, the second level was "Young Lord–in–Training." At this stage, the candidate had passed the security check and was assigned certain tasks within a ministry to develop a sense of organizational discipline. Critical to becoming a "full" Lord was a clear understanding of the 13-Point Program and Rules of Discipline, particularly that "you are a Young Lord twenty-five hours a day, no exceptions."

The third and final step was a graduation where you would receive your purple beret and be permanently assigned to an area of work. The discipline of the Young Lords helped many overcome drugs or alcohol problems. Armed with Thorazine, Valium, and canned chicken soup, many Young Lords stood watch over those who wanted to kick a heroin habit and become Lords themselves.

By now, confident of our place in the community, we expected our request for space inside the church for social programs to be seriously considered and granted. After the church's vehement refusal, and then the violent response of Reverend Carranza and the police that Sunday in December, it cleared the way for us to make our daring move. Revolution-oriented movements were becoming more vocal and militant during the autumn of 1969. One of the most notorious cases was the division of the organization Students for a Democratic Society. From the splintering of that group emerged "the Weathermen," a group that used a Bob Dylan lyric as inspiration for its name. The Weathermen engaged in covert military guerrilla actions and were to go completely underground early the next year. The Black Liberation Army, the armed wing of the Black Panther Party, was expanding and developing its capabilities. Major offensives against corporate and government targets were increasing nationally. We weren't going as far as some groups were, but planning this new type of takeover would be a first for us.

Two weeks had passed since the bloody incident and arrest in the church. We had spent those weeks inviting the community by word of mouth, leaflets, and through our recently inaugurated newspaper *Pa'lante*, to assemble at the church that Sunday. Although the "invitation" distributed by the Young Lords was not specific, our record was enough to make people suspect that something big could happen. On Sunday morning, December 28, people flooded the small church building. Then the Young Lords arrived.

Thirty Young Lords were ready for action inside the church. That was our first-line strike force. Most important, we were counting on a large number of community people who we knew would join us. We had studied the layout of the building and positioned members in key areas so that we could barricade the entire building in seconds. Only a select group of the most trusted Lords were familiar with the specifics of the entire operation.

As planned, we allowed the service to proceed without a hitch. Once it was over, I immediately stood up. That was the signal for the two main entrances and the two side exits to be sealed with fifteen-foot chains and locks. Captain of Defense Jose "Pi" Díaz and Bobby Lemus, with a small team, moved to further secure the doors. The occupation of the church was completed within minutes.

Bedlam quickly erupted among some in the congregation. Pablo informed them that they would be free to leave within a few minutes. The excitement subsided then, and we proceeded to escort out those who wanted to leave. Only about thirty people left—men, women, and children. Over two hundred people remained seated. Among those leaving was Reverend Carranza, who seemed to be in shock. Seated were Richie Perez and Luis Garden Acosta, who found the spirit of resistance and, like so many, joined the organization after the takeover.

Every major newspaper and television station sent reporters and photographers to the church. We held a press conference where we officially announced the takeover, and that we intended to use the space for a series of social programs, including free breakfasts for children, a day-care center, and free health clinics. We would also provide clothing and cultural events for the benefit of the whole community. Our message was, "Look at this church. There are two hundred fifty people from the community in this church who support what we are doing. This church is only open for three hours on Sundays, and wouldn't it be nice for it to be open five days a week with a day-care center so that parents could go to work and leave their children in a safe place? Why isn't this place feeding the hungry? Isn't that a credo of Christianity?"

That same morning Felipe presided over a meeting of the people who were still packing the main hall of the church. He explained to them the purpose of the takeover and the programs we aimed to start. There were no outbursts of enthusiasm. People remained in their seats listening attentively to what Felipe was explaining to us. Some of them nodded and made gestures of approval. This was not a show put on for them by a group of outsiders. This was to become their own "offensive," as well as the Lords'. The people knew it. In the days to come, we learned a lot together.

I was moved by their silent resolve to stay and face the consequences. My own religious feelings had mostly withered away during my years in college, replaced by a faith in revolution. I knew that most of the people did not share our revolutionary beliefs, but they did believe in something very powerful and it was compelling them to stay with us. By doing our best to teach the people to believe in themselves, we were exposing ourselves to self-reflection as well. I was feeling proud of myself for having been the one to give the signal by standing up. I "knew" about revolution, nationalism, and socialism. My belief was "scientifically based." But the congregation's belief, based on faith alone, dwarfed my action. Theirs had no explanation, no basis, and no science to back it up. And still they were resolved to continue. We were both taking leaps of faith.

While a group of Lords spoke with the remaining parishioners, another detachment of Lords secured the perimeter. The police came within hours and established a command post and security perimeter outside the church. This time the NYPD and the Tactical Police Force were very cautious. One group of Lords was assigned to remain in the church day and night, while others would come in and out, bringing supplies for the programs we would soon be setting up, and escorting people into the church to access the services. There was no immediate attempt by Reverend Carranza or the police to recover control of the building. It was a long day and a still-longer night for us. Guards were posted in lookout positions and the excitement of the first hours yielded to the hard work of organizing for the different activities we had planned. We also had time to think about how uncertain the near future was. At least I did.

Was I wasting my life? What would I do to provide for my wife and my baby? My wife was not particularly happy with me devoting all my efforts to this struggle while she was stuck with the baby and the fear of the possibility of her husband ending up in jail, or worse. She had told me many times that she was not happy with our life. Her words struck me like a hammer in the head. I knew she was right in more than one aspect. There was also this burning feeling raging inside of me. I just couldn't subdue it. There was too much injustice in my world, and something had to be done about it. Cuban composer Silivio Rodriguez described it best: "The era is delivering a newborn heart, the pain is killing her and she can take no more. We must rush to her side, for the future is at stake." Wasn't I fighting for a brighter future for my own son? Wasn't this fight for the future of all women's children? We were unable to understand each other. The takeover of the church, which felt more like a family affair with each passing moment, was an inspiration.

As soon as the story had spread throughout the city, many people showed interest in the situation. Chegüí helped by bringing to the church writer Budd Schulberg and filmmaker Elia Kazan. They came and showed the movie *The Battle of Algiers*, a classic that tells the story of the successful war for independence of that North African nation. That movie, with its depictions of popular struggle, had clear parallels to our own situation.

Tall, light black, and with a powerful smile, Chegüí did not resemble the common image of a boxer, except for his flat nose. He was always looking for the perfect joke and a good anecdote to deflate any serious debate or political dissent. Less than five years earlier, he had become the third Puerto Rican to win a world boxing championship—and light-heavyweight, at that. He was a popular hero. He hadn't been elevated to that status simply because of his skills in the ring. He was also very proud to be a Puerto Rican. The day of his first championship fight he surprised the media and everybody else, by insisting that the Puerto Rican national anthem be played before the fight for the first time ever.

His was a strange case. There he was, supporting the Young Lords, a group that advocated the independence of Puerto Rico and a socialist revolution, while he personally backed the U.S. Commonwealth in Puerto Rico—the colonial status of which we were precisely against. He certainly did not believe in the destruction of capitalism and the creation of a socialist society. He knew exactly where we were coming from, and supported us anyway. He offered us an important yet subtle, critique: Live up to the values you profess. He was unwilling to impose his beliefs on anyone, but in a very delicate fashion he was prompting us to remain consistent. That's why he'd brought Kazan and Schulberg.

The showing of the movie was only the beginning. The church, renamed by the Young Lords as "the First People's Church," was alive with its new role as the social, cultural, and political center of El Barrio. More than three thousand people came to the church over the eleven days we occupied it to get a free breakfast, clothing, or to enjoy the nightly entertainment. Here for the first time many of us heard our generation's poet laureate Pedro Petri's "Puerto Rican Obituary" and Pepe y Flora, a folklore group, performed their wonderful nationalist melodies.

With each day, the story got bigger and bigger. A real media event happened when Jane Fonda and Donald Sutherland, both co-stars of the hit movie *Klute*, showed up. The church was packed and Fonda distributed a lot of air-kisses. The people were bewildered. Jane Fonda brought Pia Lindstrom, a journalist and one of the daughters of the legendary Ingrid Bergman. We were impressed and honored by their visit, as it lent more credibility to our struggle. For us, this was a smashing propaganda success. Those two Hollywood stars were visiting the community because of the Young Lords, but above all, to show their support for the Puerto Rican community. This was more attention than we'd expected.

Sutherland kept his profile low and stuck to the role of outside supporter. Fonda was more political. She surprised us with a barrage of questions during a meeting with the leadership. "Just what do you stand for? Who are you allied with?" She was very straightforward and obviously unwilling to be used as a mere propaganda tool. We answered her questions. I think she liked our candid answers. It was very clear she felt a strong call toward political activism, later shown to the whole world by her controversial trip to Hanoi. Some years later she gave her full support to the cause of independence of Puerto Rico at a rally at Madison Square Garden.

After a few days the tension was rising, but the Central Committee did not ease up on the discipline. The consumption of alcohol and other substances was strictly forbidden, and sexual activity or similar intimacy was also out of the question, even for married couples. We were in the middle of an offensive and our strict code of conduct was enforced. Those assigned to stay overnight in the church were required to exhibit highly moral and spartan behavior.

Near the end of the first week of the takeover, city marshals appeared in the streets. Reverend Carranza had been very busy. While Young Lord guards stood still in front of the main doors, and others looked through the windows, one marshal crossed the police barricades and stood in the street. Using a bullhorn he read an injunction issued by the New York Supreme Court ordering us to vacate the building. Nobody moved and the marshals went away.

We knew what was coming next. The matter would go back for consideration by the judge, who would—we had no doubt—determine that we were in contempt of court. The following step was going to be a forcible eviction. According to what we knew about this process, it was only a matter of time before they came back. We were concerned. We had no idea how much we had pissed off City Hall and what fury the cops would wield against us in getting us out of the church.

On the tenth day, some of the Young Lords assigned to the church received orders from the Central Committee. They had been granted a pass for the whole night. That meant only two things. First, that confidential information had been received confirming that the police were going to storm the church the next day. Second, those who had received the pass were the ones assigned to come in early the next morning and be ready inside the church to get busted. It was a sobering thought. For those chosen, the usual discipline was completely lifted for the night. They could go and do whatever they wanted.

The entire organization was mobilized, except for two. Yoruba and I received strict orders not to get arrested. As minister of information, Yoruba was to handle the press the next day. As for me, the committee decided that it was in the best interests of the Young Lords to prevent my arrest and a subsequent police record; the motive behind this was my involvement in the paramilitary aspects of the organization.

It was a very long night in the church. No jokes were heard in the rooms used as quarters for the Young Lords. Some of the cadres were able to sleep, but most of them did not even try to pretend. There was widespread anticipation and concern. There were no prayers, either. At least, I did not pray—that is, unless you count sneaking a view every now and then of the sky, with the secret hope of seeing heaven. What you could mostly hear were *sotto voce* conversations about possible defensive techniques for blocking blows that would surely be thrown by the attacking police.

The next day our marching orders were very specific: Nobody was authorized to offer any resistance to the police. The faces of the Lords said it all. This was going to be a tough one. We had become accustomed to fighting back. Nobody argued. It was clear that Felipe himself and four other members of the leadership had set the example at the beginning of the Church Offensive when we endured severe blows by the police. The orders were to attempt non-violence; it was a simple matter of discipline.

At the scheduled time for me to leave the church, I looked back at my comrades who were about to be arrested. This was the first mass arrest for the Lords. My assignment was in another place. It could end up being more risky, but I could not explain it to anyone. We had trained some of the people who were to pass a real ordeal that morning. I felt that our organization was about to write one more sentence of New York's multicultural history.

At dawn, many Young Lords and supporters came to the church. When the policemen arrived, they hacked their way through the front door with axes and chain-cutters. As the cops came through the door, Juan and the lieutenant supervisor recognized each other. They were the same cops that had busted the students at Columbia University the year before. For a split second, everybody expected the worst. The first attempt at the church would surely seem like a rehearsal in comparison to the bloodbath about to begin. But it worked exactly the other way around. Once again, Juan showed his ability as a superb negotiator. A few minutes later, 103 people, including the Central Committee minus Yoruba, came out of the church with their right fists raised, marching between a corridor formed by the policemen while the crowd was singing, *"Qué bonita bandera es la bandera puertorriqueña"* ("What a beautiful flag the Puerto Rican flag is").

Then came long months of negotiations between Reverend Carranza's legal representatives and our defense attorneys. Former borough president Herman Badillo intervened in the negotiations and recommended that the charges be dropped. Sometime later, all the charges were withdrawn. Badillo and Ted Kheel did more. They mediated a settlement with the National Council of Churches and made other spaces available for our programs.

A few months later, an official report from the Methodist church conceded that "the congregation's refusal to accede to the Young Lords' demands led to a bitter conflict which ultimately involved both denominational and civic leaders." Their statement recognized the Young Lords as an organization able to represent and ignite the will of struggle within the people of El Barrio.

THE UNDERGROUND

UNKNOWN TO MANY AT THE TIME, and even today, the Young Lords had a combat-ready underground organization able to coordinate actions in New York and Puerto Rico at any time to draw attention to the colonial status of our home country and the injustices we suffered on the mainland. This secret fighting section was not the most important part of the party. Mass struggle was the paramount reason for the Young Lords' existence and success. Nevertheless, the underground played an integral role in the development of the organization, and the whole phenomenon of the Young Lords cannot be fully understood without taking it into account. The time has come to tell one part of the Young Lords' story that has never been revealed.

An unexpected defeat prompted the Lords to go ahead with

plans to recruit the underground. The idea had surfaced by the time of the takeover of the church, and this was why I was spared the responsibility of being arrested. We wanted to prevent the police from having an official, fingerprinted record of me. As days passed, other priorities, like running our social programs, consumed our immediate attention and the plan was postponed time and time again. It continued that way until we had endured a shameful encounter with an enemy with more street, political, and fire power than expected. We had recklessly put ourselves on a crash course with organized crime.

Perhaps after the astonishing victories of the Garbage, Lead, and Church Offensives we became overconfident. In politics, and personal lives as well, early triumphs can easily go to your head. After three victories in a row, we suddenly found ourselves in a real mess.

Helping young men to overcome drug addiction did not exactly make us the darlings of Barrio drug dealers. At the beginning no one paid much attention to us. With a solid market of many thousands and no real threat to their distribution points, the dealers had nothing to fear from just another community group providing an alternative for those who wanted to change their lives around and become Young Lords. After the Church Offensive, however, things began to change quickly. The community placed very high expectations on us. It seemed that everybody was expecting the next daring move of the Young Lords on behalf of the neighborhood. The heroin problem was already at epidemic proportions. Occasional marijuana users or people who consumed drugs sporadically were not at the core of the problem in the public's perception—we were in the midst of the psychedelic hippie era after all. The issue was the wasted men and women who infested the streets, often with guns, stealing to sustain their addiction. It presented a public health issue as well as a serious security threat. Many Young Lords had come from that environment and taken advantage of our rehabilitation program. Of course, after they turned their energies from crime to politics, they were no longer friendly toward their former dealers.

The problem was increased by another wave of oppression. Some corrupt police officers provided a haven for the drug traffickers and even intervened in the business. We thought that by exposing police corruption we could make a meaningful contribution to alleviate the burden of the community, but also could increase political awareness about the hypocritical role played by many of the so-called "authorities." Since we had developed good contacts with the media, we thought this would be an easy task. We hid our people with cameras in strategic locations and taped police officers making transactions with street mobsters. We really believed that journalists would see it as dynamite and unleash a political scandal. It just didn't happen. Instead of jumping all over the story and broadcasting our tape, the people we contacted at TV stations told us it was their policy not to use tapes produced by outside sources. We didn't get the message. Our ignorance was that pronounced. Instead of just stepping away, we suggested they send their own crews, and that we would direct them to the spots where the story could be gathered. Of course, the answer was no again. Then a most unexpected thing happened.

The corpse of a well-known drug dealer appeared hanging from a streetlamp. The news spread like fire. As did a rumor that the Young Lords had lynched the man in order to send a strong message to the traffickers. We tried our best to dispel the rumor, and told whoever was willing to listen that we had had nothing to do with the murder and that the guy could have been the victim of an internal turf war among the gangsters. For the first time, we realized that we were unable to get our message across. People were unconvinced. Every time one of us repeated our theory about the murder, we were met with a nod and a wink— clearly no one believed us. Soon enough we heard that someone in the mafia had put out a contract on the leaders of the Young Lords. Our chairman Felipe, in particular, had a $5,000 price tag on his head.

We tried to speak through the media again, and called a press conference to denounce the menace of the mobsters. During the press conference a journalist asked the minister of information, Yoruba, if he was pointing the finger at Italian organized crime. Fortunately enough, he did not fall into that trap. His answer was that the mafia was "an equal-opportunity employer." That was good, because at the end we eventually found out a Cuban gang was behind the contract. Besides calling public attention to the issue, there was very little else that we could do. Some of the best-trained Young Lords were assigned as bodyguards for the threatened leaders, although it was obvious they would be no match for mafia gunmen.

Yoruba's father intervened through relatives who knew how to reach intermediaries of organized crime. The gangsters wanted to negotiate directly with our "boss." In a scene resembling something out of *The Godfather*, Felipe met them and negotiated a truce. They wanted us to stop harassing their business associates and Felipe requested that they at least stop their most offensively open selling operations in the streets. At last, we could claim a very modest triumph for the community instead of going back with our bare hands.

This time there had been no massive mobilization of the community, no active involvement of common people—except for the occasional pat on the shoulder for encouragement. We had ventured alone into turf ruled by violence. It was a difficult time.

There is no mention of this whole affair in many articles about the Young Lords. Yoruba has been one of the few writers to recall it. Even I had somehow forgotten the episode. Perhaps it's because we were embarrassed to be in a situation so far over our heads. Our confidence was badly shaken by the whole experience. I think that to forget embarrassing experiences is something quite common. Using that protective mechanism, we can produce an ever-shining image of ourselves and the task of dividing the world between friends and foes becomes an easier one. Never again did the Young Lords so much as tempt another clash with organized crime. In all fairness, they complied with the truce, and afterwards, when comrades like Yoruba were sent to jail for draft evasion, they offered to protect them.

One important aspect of the lesson learned from that fiasco was that we could not continue to procrastinate over the issue of organizing a clandestine arm to the party. We had come to realize that we were working within a highly dangerous context and that we had a responsibility to the community to be ready for anything.

In the early spring of 1970, the Young Lords' underground was born. I was the commander of the underground in charge of recruiting, training, and arming our organization. My military and political rank made me an ex officio member of the Central Committee. Homage should be paid to the heroes and heroines who were always ready to sacrifice their lives in the service of political freedom, democracy, and social justice. The following are code names of real people who faced death or imprisonment, daily, by being involved: Ernesto, Blanca, Camilo, Lolita, Griselo, Celia, Oscar, Haydee, Aquila Blanca Blanca, and many others.

All of them distinguished themselves for their bravery and sincere dedication. The list is too long to mention every last one of them; it is fair to say that the level of commitment was so high that not a single soldier had to be purged from our ranks, and there were no political splits in the military.

After the First People's Church Offensive we knew that some serious collective thinking had to be done if we were to transform short-term victories into a meaningful long-range thrust toward social change. The clash with organized crime was just a catalyst. This chapter of our story begins in a mansion in Great Neck, Long Island, in one of those elegant communities with manicured lawns and beautiful estates. There, during three days in early spring of 1970, the Central Committee of the Young Lords had a retreat to reevaluate the purpose of the organization, establish a clear directive, and finalize plans for the underground.

Initially our retreat was going to be held in a place on Eighth Avenue. I was not involved in the selection of our retreat site. When Pi and I got to the area, my survival instinct went on alert immediately. This location would never work. As part of the retreat we were to go through weapons training. There was no way I would allow training to take place around the corner from a police precinct! I had to think of a quick solution. I phoned my old psychology professor at Old Westbury, and explained the situation to him, omitting some of the details. Arthur Adlerstein was very glad to hear from me, and happy to help; he made his home in Great Neck available to us. During the three-day retreat, the seven members of our committee were able to have deliberations in complete privacy—not to mention leisure—and in the evenings we would have dinner with Professor Adlerstein and his wife Adele. They were a wonderful pair of politically liberal individuals. We were grateful for their generosity.

Three major decisions were made by consensus during the

Great Neck retreat. First, we decided to promote women to the Central Committee. We didn't have much of a choice. The women's caucus had its own process of analysis, and made "a demand, not a request," according to former Lords minister of finance Denise Oliver. The women were ready to fight this one out in order to share in the decision-making process of the organization. After all, if we were to struggle for equality and justice and the creation of the "new twenty-first–century man (person)" as proposed by the immortal revolutionary master Ernesto "Che" Guevara, women demanded to be full and equal partners in the governance of the party. Women all over the world were engaged in political and military actions in defense of their homelands. The role and contribution of women in Vietnam and Cuba served as examples to our sisters in our barrios. These women put our politics to the test, and we had to put into practice what we had proclaimed to be our political truth.

The second resolution was related to the YLO national office. We decided to sever our ties with the Young Lords Organization in Chicago. Until then, we had been operating as the East Coast branch of the original, founded and based in Chicago, called the Young Lords Organization. The Chicago Lords were the result of an evolution of a street gang led by Cha-Cha Jiminez, into a high level of social and political consciousness. The founding members of the Lords in New York were mostly college dropouts, with unemployed youth, working people, and former gang members filling out the ranks. We had different working methods and the New York media at our disposal. As an organization we did not have the collective resources to maintain a national office. So we decided to go to Chicago and tell Cha-Cha and the national Central Committee that we wanted out but with camaraderie. It was a historic moment.

We all realized the separation was a risky move, and decided to go to Chicago without letting anyone there know in advance what we intended to do. All they knew was that we were coming. We had to keep the situation away from the eyes of the state. This could have been disruptive for our movement. Arriving in Chicago we went directly to National to meet our comrades. We were officially announced and were told about our living arrangements. Oddly enough, I was assigned to Omar Lopez, minister of information, Obed's brother from LADO. Later that evening we began our meeting with the national leadership. New York opened the meeting, outlining the reasons why the present arrangement of accountability was not workable for either side. Lords kept coming in and out of the room. We were on their turf. The meeting was tense, the discussion painfully truthful. We were all armed; in those days we were always armed. Some Chicago Lords felt that we had no right to split from National, let alone keep their name. The meeting went on deep into the night. Cha-Cha called for a caucus with the National Central Committee. Time started to inch along. One hour, two hours. Finally they came out. Cha-Cha stated the position. He understood our circumstances and accepted our idea of leaving the Young Lords Organization and becoming the Young Lords Party. We were all relieved, hugged and kissed each other, and got the hell out of Chicago before Cointelpro (the FBI-CIA's Counterintelligence Program) caught up with us.

On the way back to New York we acknowledged that we had won yet another victory from the state. What had just occurred in Chicago was the type of scenario created many times by the counterintelligence programs, with provocateurs and operatives, to develop an environment of distrust. It was the internal conflict and dissent that resulted in shootouts between members and led to the destruction of many organizations. It was clear to us that up until that moment in the development of the Young Lords, there had been no infiltrators in the leadership in Chicago or New York. During the ride home we talked about how Cha-Cha had single-handedly prevented the derailment—or, at worst, the destruction—of the Young Lords. His character, integrity, and credability had influenced the peaceful resolution of our parting of ways. New York and Chicago became fraternal organizations, and New York gained more respect and admiration for Cha-Cha Jiminez and the Chicago Lords. We were all Young Lords.

The third and final resolution of the Great Neck meeting was the formation of the People's Army—an arm of the organization dedicated to offensive and defensive military action under the political direction of the party. We had studied seriously the war in Vietnam, the Cuban Revolution, the African liberation movements in Mozambique, Tanzania, and South Africa, as well as the intensifying fight against Portuguese and French colonialism in Africa, and U.S. imperialism in Asia and Latin America. Although it was portrayed as a "cold war" between the United States and the Soviet Union, both powers seeking global supremacy, we did not share that view of the world's political map. From our point of view, there was a tug-of-war between reactionary capitalist forces and the peoples of the world seeking liberation, justice, and economic freedom. In that sense, the war was being fought within the United States—between those promoting militarism and those demanding independence and peace. Many youngsters who were conscripted and sent to distant countries and bloody rice fields came back home, having learned the reality of what was going on here and in Vietnam, and joined movements like the Young Lords. Their membership provided valuable combat and military experience to groups that were protesting the intrusion of U.S. military might in Southeast Asia and in the Caribbean.

Here in America in March 1970 an explosion in a bomb factory in a Greenwich Village townhouse killed three members of the Weather Underground. Two escaped. The trials of the Chicago Seven were producing sentences against the leaders of the protest movement, instead of against the police, for the 1968 Democratic National Convention riots. We knew these trials were a mockery of justice; we would later be vindicated when the convictions were overturned. For the moment, the message seemed to be very clear: Radicals had no political space in bourgeois America. Scores of black, white, Latino, Native American, and Asian activists were going underground. Donald Cox (Field Marshal of BPP), Bernadine Dohrn, William Ayers, Jeff Jones, Eleanor Stein, Assata Shakur (JoAnne Chesimard), Zayd Shakur, Francisco Torres, and many other former SDS members went under. Radical black activist Angela Davis was accused of helping Jonathon Jackson break out of jail, during which four people were killed, in August 1970. Davis escaped underground and was chased throughout the nation. She was eventually caught in New York City, but was freed eighteen months later, and ultimately all charges were dropped when a jury found no sufficient evidence to convict her. Father Daniel Berrigan, a Catholic priest from Maryland, was another high-profile person who went underground after being convicted of burning draft cards in a protest against the Vietnam War. They all made the FBI's Ten Most Wanted list.

In Southeast Asia, Vietnam was getting worse. In March, right-wing lieutenant-general Lon Nol deposed the government of Prince Sihanouk in Cambodia, whose moderate regime had been sympathetic to the liberation struggle of the people of Vietnam. General Nol began a murderous campaign of massacres of the peasants while U.S. forces took the opportunity to extend operations into that nation. The world watched in astonishment as the mighty U.S. military leveled the region.

This was taking its toll back home in America. As the war appeared to be spreading throughout the whole Southeast Asian region, turmoil erupted in the universities. "Hell no, we won't go!" became the battle cry of students across the country. The Reserve Officers Training Corps (ROTC) facilities became targets of anti-war student rage. It was only a matter of time before something really serious happened. In April of 1970, the National Guard opened fire on the students at Kent State University in Ohio, and shortly thereafter, the police did the same at Jackson State University in Mississippi. Nearly seventy-five colleges would remain closed for the rest of the year.

We supported the immediate and unconditional withdrawl of U.S. troops from Vietnam. The daily defeats of the U.S. war machine, the most sophisticated in the world, became part of our day-to-day life. Repression was not just theory—it was happening in practice everywhere. It was something experienced by Puerto Rican patriots as routine. We understood that the more success we achieved in our actions, the more repression would come in response. The deaths in 1965 of our Puerto Rican national hero Pedro Albizu Campos, and of the African-American militant leader Malcolm X, deeply affected our communities. Almost every day the press carried stories about the killing of Black Panthers in their beds while they slept. Chicago state Black Panther Party chairman Fred Hampton, a close friend of Cha-Cha Jiminez, was one of those heroes killed. It would take the city of Chicago over twenty years to pay reparations to his family. We weren't going to be killed as we slept.

We knew there would be no chance of success for a political

party like ours if we lacked a strong military wing to defend us. Minister of education Juan González was given the responsibility of organizing the ministry of defense; that Juan would be liaison to the underground was of paramount importance. As the chairman of the Student Strike Committee, he had a close relationship with many young white radical organizations including the Weather Underground. Contact with them would prove invaluable—they were already deeply involved in covert attacks on military and state installations, protesting among other things the war in Vietnam, colonialism in Puerto Rico, and the abuses and repression of Native American communities. Juan became my contact with the Central Committee.

There was also another important aspect to Juan being the individual issuing orders. He would not be an active member of the People's Army, only our political attaché. The People's Army was to be completely subordinate to the political leadership of the party—political decisions would drive the military. Being the person who had brought the core group together, it was unanimous that I would form a collective of three to command the underground. As the analysis and decision-making process progressed, my concerns grew. I was a Young Lord and a radical, but I was also trying to be a husband and a father.

My son, Miguel Albizu, and his mom had basic survival needs. Right now she was working to support all three of us while I was a full-time revolutionary. I felt guilty about burdening my wife with the responsibility of working to support the family and then coming home to take care of the baby and the apartment. I needed to help more: I needed a paying job. It was a serious conflict. The responsibility that came along with my political commitment weighed very heavily on my shoulders. This new arrangement of operating clandestinely would allow me to continue my political work *and* get a job, so I could become a better parent and contribute economically to the family. Somehow, I had to make it all work.

Shortly after we returned from Great Neck, the leadership put out the story that I had left the Young Lords because of my pressing family issues. It was the beginning of the "phase-out" strategy in my journey to live a double life—a common worker aboveground, a soldier in the underground. At least half the members believed the story. Some of them couldn't understand. It was no secret that I was in bad need of a job. We did not make a big fuss about my resignation. Nor did I completely desert the organization. A complete break surely would have raised suspicions and brought unwarranted attention from the authorities. As time went by, my story of leaving the Young Lords gained more and more credibility.

My brother-in-law, Hiram, was deputy commissioner of the Addiction Service Agency and got me a job at Lincoln Hospital's Methadone Maintenance Program. As an organization, the Young Lords were against Methadone Maintenance. The name itself has a Nazi origin. First synthesized in Germany, "Dolphine," is the generic name for methadone. It has been said that it was named after the Führer, Adolf himself. Methadone is made from a synthetic opiate base, manufactured with all of the addictive traits associated with opiates, and then some. Unable to produce enough morphine during World War Two, the Nazi pharmaceutical industry gave priority to the development of a chemically engineered product that had the same painkilling effects as morphine—methadone. In our opinion, state-sanctioned methadone maintenance programs just exchanged one addiction for another. The sole manufacturer of methadone, the Eli Lilly corporation in Puerto Rico, made huge profits converting addicts into zombies we called Methadonians. We did, nevertheless,

understand and sympathize to some extent with the use of methadone in decreasing dosages for heroin addicts who wanted to
detoxify and become drug-free. I obviously had political differences with the job, but it was the only one I could find and I
was lucky to have it. Eventually the Young Lords would establish
our own acupuncture-based detox program.

My life had changed. I would leave for work in the morning,
an almost picture-perfect image of the typical family man. In
reality I was far from typical and very, very busy. With only a
small budget from the Young Lords I had to establish my cover,
and organize the infrastructure of the People's underground. My
first priority was to rent a series of apartments located within
our community. The other two members of the underground
leadership, a man and a woman, would pose as a newly married
couple and rent an apartment. These we established as safe
houses. One of them was designed for headquarters; the others
were for the storage of weapons, ammunition, and supplies, and
as medical and training facilities.

The apartments were adequately furnished so that if an unexpected visitor arrived, nothing would be revealed. Some of the
items were hidden behind false walls. It was—again—on-the-job
training. We were all very creative.

It was odd to go to several real-estate agencies and sign con-
tracts for apartments and then take measurements in order to go
to the hardware store and do much of the remodeling work. In
situations like this, you learn how minor details are of importance. To contract someone to do the work would be out of the
question. We could not risk the whole operation because a car-
penter had suspicions or had asked questions. So the hammer,
screwdriver, and paintbrush became the first weapons in the underground army and the first drills were doing masonry and
painting. It's tiresome to take care of the maintenance of

one apartment; overseeing the remodeling and repairs of several apartments made me feel like an overworked superintendent.

During those days I felt a strange sense of relief. I was overworked, but being constantly busy prevented me from worrying or overthinking things too much. I had a lot of work and endless hours keeping up with my job in the hospital and meeting with the leadership of the underground. As soon as my workday was finished at the hospital, I had to rush to apartments all over the city to continue with my newly acquired job as repairman. All of it was so absorbing that there was little time left for dealing with negative thoughts about anything. Actually, there was not time for indulging in thinking at all. I began to enjoy it, and discovered the therapeutic pleasure of that intense physical activity. Without realizing it, I began to behave as my father had when I was a boy. I would go back to my home at night, spend a little time with Mutin and Miguel Albizu, eat chicken curry and listen to Machito, Puente, Palmieri, Barretto—along with Emerson, Lake and Palmer, Chicago, Sweetwater, Ten Wheel Drive, the Band, Mandrill, Santana—before dropping into bed. Things were moving very fast.

Soon enough I received notice from Juan that contact with the Weather Underground had been made. I was to meet one of the underground Weather people at a clandestine location. I was excited. I knew, from that moment on, I wouldn't just be living a double life, I would be courting the possibility of exposure every single day. Making contact with another underground organization opens the door wide for trouble. A heightened state of vigilance was my only guiding light for survival.

Preparation for the first meeting was thorough; nothing was to be left to chance. In this case, the need to avoid "a deadly mistake" was not a just a figure of speech. At the same time that I was quickly developing a sense that all my movements had to be carefully calculated, I also had to learn the exact opposite principle—to trust others. Our survival depended on it. I had to trust a person I had never met. Since I was living in the open with a hidden life, while they were fully underground and could be arrested or killed on sight, there was no choice but to leave my security in their hands.

The date was fixed for the meeting. I arrived at the exact hour ordered in the message. The person was already there, a man. No one would have discerned anything strange about him. That lack of impressiveness was what impressed me the most. There is a strict protocol in the underground before contact. We watched each other from a distance, making certain that neither one of us had brought a tail. Satisfied that it was safe, he took me to one of their safe homes. Greeted at the door by an unknown woman, we began the exchange of gifts.

I can't remember what he gave to me. At one point I was given a metal ring carved from a piece of a downed U.S. aircraft. I am not sure if that trophy was given to me in the first meeting or in one of the many I would have during my underground years. I do remember that I gave him a picture of Don Pedro Albizu Campos. He accepted my gift with appreciation.

During that first meeting I was also given instructions for a future meeting. First, they would always contact me and I would go to whatever place they chose. If for any reason the meeting was canceled without prior notice—not a common occurrence—there was always a backup plan. Whenever a meeting didn't happen, my concern skyrocketed. This was our revolution. We were in control. I had to wait the best I could until the fifteenth of the next month, and then go to a certain library and pick up a specific book that was on a designated shelf. Inside were instructions for the next meeting.

After the meetings, I would go home, to my wife and Miguel

Albizu. Mutin never knew the details of my work. Our marriage was quickly coming to an end. My inability to build an intimate relationship was symptomatic of my early childhood trauma. Also, I had not been faithful in my marriage. It was not just the guilt of my indiscretion, but the fact that my guilt lived in my conscience. This is a place in life that moves you to resolve the daily lies and deceit. Whether in politics or in personal relationships, only the truth, the complete truth, can bring forth forgiveness. I took a chance and told Mutin about my philandering. I was willing to accept the consequences. We would either work it out or it would be the end. It was the end. In 1971 Mutin and I would ultimately separate. We, each in our own way, have attempted to be a positive and guiding influence in Miguel's life. I was alone in my double life, working and building the underground.

We felt that our military mission would be more effective by targeting some of the government installations and multinational companies exploiting our people. Recruiting stations and corporate headquarters were high on our list. The assistance of the Weather Underground was very important. They would give us technical support and training for the assembly, storage, and use of explosives. I was trained first and in turn I trained the other members.

The army was organized into cells, operating independently from each other, with intercell contact as minimal as possible. Each cell had to be properly trained in reconnaissance, information-gathering, planning, explosives, weapons, medical capacity, and news media. Recruits would also go to upstate New York to train with different types of firearms in designated shooting clubs. There was also the prerequisite of taking an oath to commit their lives for the cause. For the Young Lords, every step was discussed and calculated as a group. It was done not just to survive, but to win a victory for the people. We were sustained by this belief and we were not only willing, but expecting, to donate our lives in the process of revolution. The oath was taken very seriously by each and every one of us.

For the soldiers, the sanctity of the oath was even more pressing. We were not only exposed to the same threats as all the other Young Lords' leaders and cadres; but we were to protect, to defend, and to risk our lives in direct action whenever necessary or when ordered to do so. Nothing in the life of a soldier was more serious than his or her oath. History shows with shame and discomfort how many young people just like us throughout Latin America, from the same backgrounds, organizations, and political beliefs, were kidnapped and never heard from again. Thousands of our counterparts became known as "Los Desaparecidos" or "The Disappeared." Thirty years later mass graves of disappeared are still being discovered.

By September 1970 we had the basics, including some organized cells, and we were almost ready to begin the general recruitment drive. Although most of my time that summer was consumed with the underground, the above ground Young Lords was combating another deadly health epidemic plaguing El Barrio.

THE HIJACK

THE NEWS REACHED El Barrio at lightning speed: We were facing a tuberculosis outbreak. For months we had been doing PPD testing for TB in the tenement buildings and public housing in El Barrio; we knew the crisis was going to explode soon, and the Young Lords would have the responsibility to respond.

The story had not appeared in any local newspapers. There was no official warning or statement. Still, we knew what was going on—if you lived there, you couldn't *not* know what was going on. Hundreds of people from East Harlem—our friends, neighbors, and relatives—were being treated for the deadly disease at local hospitals. We also knew many of the health-care workers in the area—all Puerto Rican. They confirmed our suspicions. With all of these people in the know, it wasn't long

before the Latino community knew about the impending outbreak. Word of mouth, like brushfire, spread the details to every
corner of El Barrio, including our headquarters at 111th Street
and Madison, in no time. We conducted our own investigation
to confirm people's suspicions, and by June of 1970 we realized
they were justified. We were in for a huge health crisis. We hit
the streets again, this time to fight for our collective right to
decent and affordable health care.

Hospitals, especially those serving the poor, had not established adequate preventive health-care programs. There was no
significant outreach agenda to protect the community from com-
municable diseases. This, we concluded, was a dangerous and vicious circle of brutal neglect that seemed absolutely unnecessary.
Overworked, marginally employed, and surviving on meager welfare checks, our poor, duty-bound men and women were forced to
live in rotten tenements and, victimized by their political environment and the wealthy, becoming easy prey for extremely dangerous diseases. Without proper warnings and preventive care,
tuberculosis victims were themselves infecting their own families
and neighbors, and many didn't recognize the symptoms or understand the necessity of getting immediate treatment. Too many
people waited until they were coughing up blood and in severe
pain before going to the emergency rooms.

In order to curb the outbreak we had to test everyone at risk.
It wouldn't be easy, but it was doable, and the only option available to us. Testing was available at a health clinic downtown, but
few people went; it was too inconvenient. The test required two
trips: first to have the skin pierced with a needle covered with a
biological re-agent, and then a second trip a few days later for a
health-care worker to measure the bump produced under the
skin and decide if the reaction was negative or positive. Even

after all of this, the test was inconclusive. If the result was positive, then a chest X ray was necessary to confirm the diagnosis. At first the Young Lords presumed that this was a minor burden, considering the deadly dangers of the illness. But for people supporting families on limited incomes, dependent on hourly wages and with no "annual leave" time, it was a major burden. Convincing people to visit the clinic would be near impossible; instead, we decided to bring the clinic to them.

Progressive doctors throughout the city gave the PPD skin tests to us and trained us to administer them to our people. Only with their help were we able to persuade the community to get tested and save their own lives. Skin testing was the first step; the second was to provide a chest X ray for those who had tested positive. We weren't prepared for the large numbers of people who would require the test. We needed a better plan to deal with the overwhelming numbers.

We heard that the city had a mobile X-ray truck. The unit was reportedly making rounds in the five boroughs. Their procedure was very simple. The truck would go to a neighborhood, park on a street, and test anyone who was interested. The only problem was, we didn't know when the mobile truck would reach our area, and we had an emergency on our hands.

A delegation of the Young Lords was sent to the City Health Department's main office near City Hall, at 125 Worth Street. The small group had been instructed to request information regarding the schedule of the mobile truck in order to have enough time to mimeograph and distribute flyers to inform the public of the date the truck would be in El Barrio, as well as the location and details of the procedure. We also requested that the truck be parked near our offices. The political gain of having the mobile unit in front of the organization's headquarters was obvious. In all honesty, that was not our motivation. We just wanted the truck to be in an area familiar to everyone since the 1950s, when the legendary Puerto Rican street gang the Viceroys, had centered its turf on that block. The area had also served in the 1960s as the field base for the Real Great Society, and its anti-poverty shock troops.

On the date of the meeting with the officials in charge of routing the mobile truck, our delegates dressed in what we considered appropriate attire to impress the government bureaucrats. We had our Young Lords purple berets, T-shirts and buttons depicting our slogan. You can imagine the impression it made on the three middle-aged white bureaucrats who showed up. They agreed to meet our delegation, but it then became evident that those three arrogant characters had no interest in our proposal.

We were pissed when the delegates presented their report during a general meeting with the Central Committee. The city officials had dismissed our request that they should change their existing policy and give advance notice of the mobile X-ray truck location. The official responses to our pleas: "This is how we've always done business in this department," and "We don't have the money to change it."

We were in shock! An outbreak of a very contagious and highly dangerous disease was taking place in the New York area and the agency in charge of public health refused to accept co-operation offered by members of that very community. Not only had they issued no warnings to the people, but they didn't want us to distribute flyers informing the afflicted when and where to go. Their feeling was that any individual who wanted to know the location of the mobile lab on any given day had to phone the Department of Health. It was not only an inefficient method, but a criminal one. No responsible public official could believe that such a system would be effective in a community where most people lacked a telephone or knew little English.

As in the Garbage and Church Offensives, the Young Lords decided it was time to take things into our own hands. This time, Juan González would take the lead.

"Appropriate the truck," he said.

Further explanation was unnecessary. Everyone nodded in agreement before he was able to utter another word.

Being one of the senior officers, along with Pi, in the defense ministry, I knew what would come next; the Central Committee had assigned us to lead the operation. Within hours, a task-force team from our ministry of defense started to work on a plan to hijack the mobile X-ray truck. We would not be dealing with the misappropriation of shoddy brooms. This was an expensive high-tech piece of equipment. Some five or six law violations—most of them felonious—would be committed if we were caught in the process of carrying out the operation.

The plan was to conduct a swift but smooth takeover of the mobile facility in broad daylight on a busy street, and bring it to a preselected location. It was a daring plan and, because it was so bold and audacious, would serve as another media event and urban legend that would eventually paint El Barrio as the Sherwood Forest for oppressed Puerto Ricans in the United States. Every detail of the plan had been carefully worked out. Or so I thought.

It began simply enough. We called the health department, just as any individual was expected to do, and asked for the schedule of the X-ray truck. By repeating that for several days, we were able to figure out the truck's route. Then we sent out a small information-gathering team. We learned all the details of the standard procedure followed by the people in charge of the truck. The reconnaissance operation provided us with enough information to arrange the hijack. The brothers reported that the mobile X-ray truck was always parked on a corner, and that there were no police or security guards assigned to it. Those two details meant there would be no parked cars in front of the truck, blocking the getaway after the unit was seized. If we moved swiftly and without attracting too much attention from people passing by, we would not have to engage police forces—at least not during the first phase of the operation.

Two technicians were the whole crew. They traveled in the front cabin of the truck, and after it was parked in the designated corner, they would step down, open a door, unfold a staircase, and stay inside the cargo container that had been turned into a lab. The two technicians would sit inside, not particularly aware of their surroundings, and just wait for people to come in for X-ray tests. Since the communities had no advance notice and no effort had been made for any outreach, there were no waiting lines and every now and then someone would go inside, one at a time.

Pi and I figured that the seizure of the mobile truck could be executed without any struggles. We selected one additional member to be part of the assault team. His name was Huey, a young Puerto Rican who looked like the twin brother of Huey P. Newton, the legendary leader of the Black Panthers. Although Pi and Huey were among our youngest members, no more than sixteen years old, both were highly regarded political cadres of the organization. We were also all skilled in martial arts. They were both intense, wiry with olive complexions and thick eyebrows. It was invigorating to see Pi in action. He moved with the grace of a jaguar stalking its prey, and attacked with deadly accuracy. Huey studied kung fu. He could harness raw energy into soft, deadly, precise moves with the grace of the wind.

Japanese nunchakus were our only weapons. They are very versatile as a defensive and offensive weapon in hand-to-hand combat and, in the hands of a skilled fighter, nunchakus can inflict a range of damage, from death to slight injury. In this case, we were to carry them strictly for defense, and use them only as a last resort. All the intelligence gathered made us confident that the hijack could be executed without any serious difficulty.

To make things even easier, I had appropriated three long white labcoats from a closet at the New York Blood Bank, where I worked as part of my "phasing out" of the organization. There was, however, an important part of the plan that had to be carried out with utmost care. We needed the full cooperation of the lab technicians. We knew that to subdue them with the threat of force was easy. Since we had no lab technicians among us, we had to somehow persuade those guys to understand and work with us in administering the X-ray tests, otherwise the whole operation would be useless. Our intent was to establish a connection with our captives at once. We practiced what we would say to them. We wanted to convey our humanness and respect for life, as well as guarantee their safety.

We rehearsed the script time and time again. Pi was to tell the technicians: "We'd really like you to stay with us and x-ray our people. Once we get to where we are going, if you really want to leave, that's fine. We don't intend to hurt anybody in our effort." Then Huey was to add: "We have a lot of people who have tested positive and really need to be x-rayed." It was paramount to make the technicians confident they wouldn't be harmed. After all, they were not our enemies; we wanted to embarrass their employers. It was also important for us to make them believe that we were merely going to relocate the truck to a place where they could better serve our community. The plan included approaching them respectfully and politely, but with resolve.

Finally we received notice that the truck would be at 116th Street and Lexington Avenue in a couple of days. The area, near the big marketplace known as "*la marqueta,*" was the busiest and one of the most colorful commercial spots in El Barrio—the heart of East Harlem. If your aim was to show off the city's resources and give the impression that you were doing something positive for the people, then it was an excellent location. If you really wanted to go farther than the public-relations scenario, and attract the people that need to be tested and conduct the lab operation in an orderly and efficient fashion, you needed to go somewhere else. We were ready to remedy that bureaucratic miscalculation.

Yoruba contacted the newspapers, radio, and television stations, and told them to send their reporters and crews to our headquarters at 111th Street the next day—about an hour before we planned to begin administering the tests. Meanwhile, we moved fast and contacted every single person who had tested positive for TB and told them to come early in the morning for X-ray tests. With everything seemingly under control, we had to produce the truck. Nothing could go wrong.

When we got to the area that morning, it was easy to know the exact place where the truck was to be parked, because the police had cordoned off a spot on one of the corners early in the morning. No buttons, no berets, no field jackets. We just waited half a block below the southwest corner of 115th Street and Lexington Avenue. We each had our lab coats under our arms.

Soon enough, the truck appeared. It was enormous. That vehicle was thirty-plus feet long, with two axles and ten wheels, and must have weighed ten to twelve tons. I had never commandeered such a huge truck. It made my old Volkswagen look like an ant. Calculating this truck's dimensions should have been enough for me to realize that something might go wrong. I tried to remain cool.

When the truck, was finally parked, the two technicians stepped down from the cabin and approached the patients' entrance on the curb side of the van. In an almost mechanical way, they opened the door, unfolded the staircase, and went inside.

As we approached the truck, we unfolded our white coats. Clad in lab coats and looking like medical professionals, we walked toward the truck. Pi and Huey rushed inside, while I waited outside trying to look nonchalant. I could imagine the surprise for those two white men, one white-haired and the other middle-aged, with our unexpected visit.

Since I was standing several feet away outside and they were inside the van, I was unable to hear or see if Pi and Huey were following the script. Whatever they actually did and said, it worked. A few minutes later Pi opened the side door enough to throw the keys to me, and then closed the door. I don't know if I was being affected by the excitement of the operation, juvenile enthusiasm, or plain wishful thinking, but I remained completely focused on our step-by-step plan and paid no attention to the size of the vehicle I was supposed to drive. There was no time for private fears. The time for action was strictly established and the three of us had to move with precision. I climbed into the cabin and started to drive. Later I was told that during the five or six minutes' drive from 116th Street and Lexington to 111th Street and Madison, they provided the two technicians with a small political briefing about what was going on in El Barrio, and our purpose for helping our people.

As I sat in front of the steering wheel I realized what a serious mistake it was for me to think that I could drive this truck. I should have ordered the technician/driver to drive while I kept a watchful eye on him. But I was in the driver's seat now and we had to get moving. After a minute of inspecting the dashboard, I started the truck. Under my unskilled command, the machine moved onto Lexington and I stopped it a block later for a red light at 115th Street, facing west. Looking into the side mirrors as much as possible to make sure the police were not chasing us, I drove very slowly. Going straight ahead was easy, but turning corners was near impossible. The truck was so heavy and long that it required me to swing very wide.

While making a left onto Park Avenue going south, I turned short and the back tires came over the curb and across the sidewalk. It happened so fast that I had no time to stop. The screeching of the tires pierced my ears, and the crunching of splintering wood ran through my spine while cold sweat poured from my body. I glanced fearfully at a side-view mirror and saw a kaleidoscope of ice, cups, and brightly hued syrup flying through the air. I felt sick, overcome by shame and fear. Yet, to see the image of an old man standing amid the wreckage of his *piragüa* cart and pointing an accusing finger at me, was somewhat of a relief. Nobody had been injured. As the image of the accusing man grew smaller in the mirror, so did my own image, in my conscience. My carelessness had caused someone to suffer. I would have to take full responsibility for it later. But there was no time to stop now.

A few minutes after the accident, we pulled up across the street from our office at 111th Street. There were at least fifty people waiting on the sidewalk. As I set the brake and jumped out, Pi and Huey opened the side door and unfolded the stairway. Immediately the people lined up for the tests, and many Young Lords in berets surrounded the truck and proceeded to tape placards up all over it proclaiming, "HEALTH CARE IS A RIGHT, NOT A PRIVILEGE," and "FREE PUERTO RICO." Puerto Rican flags were the final touch.

The street was soon swarmed with newspeople, with microphones and cameras, as well as at least fifteen police cars. We barricaded the truck with garbage cans and parked cars next to it to prevent an easy removal of the truck by the police. Several helicopters circled the area. It was intimidating but we knew the police did not want to risk a riot by moving against the growing crowd. Health Department officials also showed up and were astonished by the large number of people who came to get tested, and the militancy of the community. We again created a political situation that paralyzed the police. They had no choice but to steer clear so that people could get their X rays.

As for the two technicians, the story unfolded quite well. At first they reacted with skepticism, especially the older, white-haired one, but we did our best to ease tensions by offering cold drinks. What really put them at ease was the reaction of the people. After going from borough to borough with the truck in what appeared to be a fruitless task, they finally felt appreciated and respected. Juan estimated that over 150 people were given X-ray tests that day. The technicians told us that the previous day they had provided the same service for only thirty people.

Once everything was settled with the technicians, I was able to think about the *piragüa* accident. I looked for Denise Oliver, the minister of finance, and, after explaining to her about the accident, I requested $50. That was a pretty large sum for our organization at the time. Denise didn't ask too many questions. We just walked into the office and she gave me the money in cash. Then I hurried back to the corner of the accident.

When I was trotting toward the area, I saw the old man walking toward me. A young woman, about my age, was with him. It was his daughter. A block away, the man recognized me and picked up his pace while pointing an angry finger in my direction. He was steaming-mad when we met, but the young woman was the first to talk.

"You could have killed my father," she snapped.

"I'm really sorry," I replied, meaning it. "But he wasn't hurt, it was only the cart . . . and I'm very sorry about that. It was my fault, I was careless, I apologize."

Without waiting for their reply, I handed the man the fifty dollars. He trembled a little when he was taking the money. In those days, it was a large sum, enough to pay for labor and materials to rebuild his cart, to make up for the few days that would pass before he would be back in business, and enough even to buy a few blocks of ice. The man calmed down and went on his way, his daughter looking satisfied with the deal. I remained alone on the sidewalk, alone with myself.

Even after compensating the man, I felt bad. To destroy someone's means of earning a living and feeding his family is a serious crime. Revolutionary ideology is not enough. To be a revolutionary is a flesh-and-soul commitment for the betterment of a people. Some things cannot be paid for with money.

For me, as a Puerto Rican born and raised in New York, a *piragüa* pushcart vendor is someone very special. He represents an important part of our culture. Those shaved-ice cones filled with Caribbean tropical fruit syrups, not only ease the body during the hot summer, their sweet goodness reminds us of who we are and where we come from, without words. I once sold *piragüa* for a summer, working for a man who owned a bakery. It only lasted a few months, but what a summer! I found out what it feels like to always have cold hands because of the work. I learned to use the heavy blade to scrape small quantities of ice from a large ice-block into a receptacle, shovel it into a paper cup, then press a funnel into the ice to make a little cone-shaped place to pour the syrup. Once in a while, I'd get real fancy and zip a little straw into the ice before handing it to a customer.

I don't know who invented the *piragüa*—why it was done or how. I do know, however, that it is a pleasure of my culture to down a *piragüa* in the middle of summer. We can go all the way back to ancient times, to the tribes that created Judaism and Christianity and, later, Islam. In *Arabian Nights*, we can read about the water vendors in Middle Eastern cities. It was common for them to add the scent of roses or other flavors to the water, to make it more pleasurable. In that immense geography, you can watch snowy peaks in the distance while your bare feet endure the heat of the desert. The whole idea of the conical top of a mountain covered with snow and ice might have given anyone the idea for this simple treat. In our ancient homeland the Taínos traveled on water in carved-out tree trunks they called *piragüa*.

Perhaps this is just a fanciful thing on my part but, whatever the origins of *piragüa*, the fact remains that it is a humble food, most likely created by the poor as a way of making the essential act of drinking water a special pleasure. Flavored syrup adds a burst of color and taste, transforming bland water into a treat, like candy. It may not seem like much, but in El Barrio, affordable little pleasures like these were few and far between, making the *piragüa* man even more valued in my community. *Piragüa* became an essential thread in the cultural fabric. It reminds me of the humble hamburger, a staple of the American diet and a cultural symbol second only to apple pie. Few people know that the hamburger was created by poor immigrants traveling to the United States on Hamburg Line steamships. The meat they were given on the journey was so bad that the only way the unfortunate passengers could swallow it was by grinding it down and sandwiching it between two halves of bread. This habit endured among the poor for decades, as part of their voyage to freedom.

It wasn't until the early twentieth century that the "hamburger" made its official debut at the St. Louis World's Fair, and people lined up willingly to pay for it. It was a success, of course. *Piragüa* tells a similar story of persevering—and triumphing—over adversity. Because it embodies the revolutionary spirit I believe in so much, the destruction of this man's cart affected me deeply.

There was something else, too. Working as a *piraguero* for that brief time had shown me the joy such work could bring to others. Making something with my hands that brought a smile to someone's face, gave me a unique feeling. Even though I only worked for a short time, the experience left an imprint on my character, and on my approach to life. I didn't toil in the *piragüa* trade, but I had been a *piraguero* in training. That day, because of my poor judgment and sloppiness, I had failed the master.

I can still see the face of the *piraguero* and his accusatory finger. I am grateful he accepted the compensation I offered, but I regret that we were unable to have a talk, from a veteran *piraguero* to an apprentice.

"THE BUTCHER SHOP"—LINCOLN HOSPITAL

TO REFER to the first Lincoln Hospital in the Bronx as "old" would be unfair. The word *old* should be reserved for persons or things that grow better, more cherished, or more dignified with time— like old parents, old friends, or old loves. That was certainly not the case with the institution that in the 1970s had become the worst health-care facility not just in the Bronx, but in the city.

The borough was already over 60 percent Puerto Rican. In less than a decade, hundreds of thousands of Puerto Ricans had "crossed" the Harlem River and moved into tenements. The Bronx was rapidly becoming a large slum area. Several factors contributed to this. The majority of the Puerto Ricans moving to the area were not entrepreneurs, but blue-collar workers, often without jobs. That meant the area was considered less valuable and there was little investment, public or private, to provide for the needs of the people. Lacking the long-term sense of community and history present in East Harlem, the newly formed Puerto Rican neighborhood in the Bronx had less power and fewer institutions to attract government attention or to defend themselves from abuses.

The word to describe what was going on would have been "neglect." As a matter of fact, that attitude of neglect toward the Bronx had started before the arrival of the Puerto Ricans, and is what made it possible for thousands of my people to obtain low-rent apartments in the area.

For the Bronx itself, this had been a long path into oblivion and decay. It seemed like quite a different place than the fertile land in which, centuries ago, the Swedish captain Bronck had established a farm. The area had always carried the mark of workers, especially poor migrant workers. Several languages and cultures formed the mosaic of agricultural laborers, mostly white European. In due time, the groups that prevailed were the Irish Catholics and European Jews. The farmland, fertile and separated from Manhattan only by the Harlem River, became rich by supplying the goods to ever-growing New York. After the American Revolution, the area was even considered as a candidate to become the nation's capital.

With the end of the Second World War, however, things began to change for the Bronx. Factories were leaving New York in search of cheap labor elsewhere. Highly skilled workers left for the suburbs of New Jersey. At the same time, displaced African-Americans were rushing into Northern cities and displaced Puerto Ricans were taking advantage of a surplus of cheap airline tickets to escape their misery on the island, then regarded as the poorhouse of the Caribbean. While war veterans who could afford to move went into new housing projects like Levittown, the less fortunate moved into the already decaying tenements of areas like the Bronx.

Then, the Bronx was battered by post-war decline. The American economy had boomed during the war years, producing goods for the war effort as well as Europe. As goods were consumed overseas, factories produced more and more to keep up with the continuous demand. The manufacturing effort turned to the domestic market, making refrigerators, cars, washing machines, and other appliances affordable to a growing affluent, working and middle class. Advertisers promoted the rapid consumption of goods. Consumerist society was born.

Unfortunately, this boom for many manufacturing centers in the country passed right by the Bronx. This new capitalist offensive actually worsened the already difficult economy by breeding contempt and resentment among the newly displaced workers unable to earn a living wage who could not participate as consumers. Having to take your shoes to the shoe-repair shop instead of just discarding them and buying new ones, indicated your class status. Bitterness grew among those once hard-toiling workers who were now denied access to the new freedom: the freedom to consume.

Society provided alternatives for those outside of the work force. The government established a mammoth provisional relief system that quickly turned permanent in order to provide food, money, and rent for those in need. The streets provided heroin and other drugs as a substitute for the hard realities of life; they created a physical dependency and a false sense of tranquility.

Under these conditions, crime soared and many old Bronx residents fled. It became increasingly more like a war zone than a neighborhood—abandoned buildings dominated the landscape. The Bronx was among the most devastated urban zones of this period. While much of the country thrived, the Bronx entered a notorious decline, overlooked by many who thought it better to just ignore it.

Of the several Puerto Rican communities in the Bronx, most affected by that neglect was the South Bronx. In time, the area would become a shameful symbol of urban decay at its most horrific. Dilapidated and burned buildings gave the area a bombed-out look. Park areas had turned into rats' nests and wastelands. Crime seemed to be the only important trade going on in the area, while thousands of residents tried to eke out a living and survive.

The only word to explain the cause of such a disaster is "neglect," and the old Lincoln Hospital is a good example. The five-building redbrick complex of the hospital, founded in 1839, was declared obsolete back in 1949. Bronx folk legend has it that former slaves received medical care there. It was eleven years later, in 1961, that they condemned the building and the city approved the budget for the construction of a new hospital. The hospital was allowed to remain open for the poor (black and Puerto Rican) communities who would be served by an apprentice medical staff (interns and residents).

By 1970 the northeast cornerstone had not been laid. This was due to a legal battle between the city and a plastics factory that refused to relocate and continued to operate on the plot of land designated for the new health facility. After more than twenty years of waiting for their new hospital, Bronx residents in the area were growing restless. The decrepit buildings, declining quality of health care, and abusive attitudes by non-Spanish-speaking doctors, posed a serious health threat to patients. This list of complaints was growing daily and it was time for the Young Lords to get involved.

Almost a year had passed since the announcement of the formation of the new group and we were very busy working, not only in East Harlem, but in several Puerto Rican and New York communities. The Bronx and Lower East Side branches were the first outside of El Barrio. Newark, Bridgeport, Boston, and Philadelphia quickly followed. From the Garbage Offensive in July 1969 to the hijack of the mobile X-ray truck in June 1970, our efficiency and thoroughness in promoting people's politics had greatly developed. Yoruba and I established the Bronx branch. It would be the Latino Information Center where *Pa'lante* would be laid out for printing. We also intended to focus on Lincoln Hospital. At the hospital we met Cleo Silvers and Danny Argoté of the "Think Lincoln Committee" who represented health-care workers and community interests. We introduced them to members of the Health Revolutionary Unity Movement; the H.RUM news organ *For the People's Health* was distributed citywide.

The Think Lincoln Committee, H.RUM, and the Young Lords called for a rally to protest the Lincoln Hospital crisis and the lack of action by the city government. It was intended to make our presence and our dissatisfaction known, and to demand that the authorities do their job. The police interpreted the affair differently. Fifteen people were arrested and ended up with injuries from the cops. Later the police tried to claim that the protesters had provoked them, but everyone saw what really happened and knew the truth.

We responded with a rally organized by the Think Lincoln Committee. Before an estimated crowd of three hundred people we announced our platform and insisted that steps should be taken to guarantee "worker-community control of the hospital." Widely publicized by the press, our stance may have been misinterpreted as mere rhetoric. We meant business—this wasn't a ticket we couldn't cash. Our statement hinted that steps were being taken for a takeover. We were working with the community to prepare the logistics and details for the operation.

The military challenge was clear. The most important aspect was how to get the cadres into the hospital. A large detachment of the Young Lords had to reach the hospital and establish full control of the perimeter without being detected by the police or hospital security—not an easy task considering our goals weren't exactly top-secret. After the two well attended rallies, we were under constant surveillance.

Truck driver Johnny Rodriguez went to a commercial car rental company in Manhattan and got a very large moving truck. When he arrived before dawn at the designated rendezvous point—an Upper West Side apartment—our troops were already there. All of them had specific orders to show up at the meeting place and to not leave the premises until the beginning of the operation. The weapons assigned were nunchakus and Chinese stars, in order to give us some leverage in case of hand-to-hand combat with the cops. As soon as the truck was parked outside, most people rushed to climb into the back and the doors were closed. Before the truck pulled out into the avenue, two cars of the Defense Ministry (I was driving one of them) took the lead, and in less than three minutes the small convoy was on its way to the Bronx.

When the two scout cars got to the hospital, we checked the ramp that led to the emergency room and the nurses' residence to make sure that the area was "clear." At 5:30 A.M. everything was quiet. Not even one of those sleepy watchmen was around the place. Then we gave the "all clear" sign to the truck that was waiting a short distance away. The transport climbed the ramp backwards and turned in the direction of the nurses' residence, connected by a ramp to the main hospital building. When it was positioned in front of the main entrance, the back doors of the truck were opened, and the Lords, along with members of H.RUM and the Think Lincoln Committee, stepped down and rushed inside. We had studied the floor plans of the hospital and everyone moved quickly to their assigned posts. In less than five minutes, the main floor and the nurses' auditorium were secured, giving us complete control of the entrances. The mobile team went and began to inform people in the nurses' residence that we had taken over the facility and that they would have to evacuate. Many people left peacefully. The small number remaining were told to stay out of the way, and that if they were caught doing anything to compromise the takeover they would be immediately escorted out. Some twenty minutes later, the whole building was under our control and a Puerto Rican flag was raised, facing Bruckner Boulevard. We christened the hospital "the People's Hospital." Immediately after the takeover, we called the media to announce our morning press conference. The next day, *The New York Times* announced that on July 14, at 5:15 A.M., a hundred and fifty Young Lords had "invaded" the Lincoln Hospital School of Nursing at 141st Street and Bruckner Boulevard.

"We are here with nothing but love for our people," Yoruba proclaimed at the opening of the press conference. Since we were already good copy for the press, his announcement reached the whole nation. The message was based on the fact that reality could no longer be denied: "People were dying at Lincoln Hospital." It was already nicknamed "the butcher's shop."

Well before noon, hundreds of people, mostly youths, had approached the hospital to know firsthand what was going on and to join efforts with the Young Lords and the coalition. The police, of course, were also represented, with uniformed and plainclothes officers, as well as the Tactical Police Force units with all their armor. It was a potentially volatile combination. If our daring operation to take full control of the building was a surprise, what happened next was even more astonishing, and most likely prevented a bloodbath.

A new director, Dr. Antero Lacot, had been appointed two weeks earlier as the director for Lincoln Hospital and he took the opportunity to make a statement. "Because of years of neglect," he said, "we have been suffering, and now we are trying to remedy the situation. We need the cooperation of all segments of the community. We cannot do the job overnight." His statement opened the door for negotiations right away. The police officers would have to wait.

While our security forces prevented anyone without legitimate business in the hospital from getting inside, Dr. Lacot and a few members of his staff met with the leaders of the Young Lords and the coalition to review a lengthy list of demands we had composed. Shortly after four in the afternoon, Dr. Lacot emerged to announce that negotiations to work on the details would resume later, but that a fundamental agreement about the reforms had been reached. The Young Lords were to peacefully vacate the hospital but would be given permission to establish a "complaint table" for workers and patients. Also, Dr. Lacot assured workers that nobody would be fired for participating in the takeover.

After his statement, the police made their first aggressive move by interfering with one of the Young Lords who was assigned to check the credentials of everybody attempting to enter the building. It was obvious they were not ready to let Dr. Lacot and the Young Lords have it our way without some form of confrontation. The press was still milling around from the morning briefing, knowing damn sure that this story was evolving every moment. We called for a news conference to tell everybody that we were ready to leave but not by force. The tension thermometer reached a new level, as did the attention paid to us by the news media. That announcement was part of a plan designed to divert the police.

While the press conference was under way I directed Young Lords secretly out of the building. We left the building the same way we had entered it—unnoticed. More than one hundred Young Lords, H.RUM, and Think Lincoln Committee members just disappeared right under their badges. Some jumped out of windows, while others used the most unexpected gates to exit the building. Another detachment officially left the building through the front door, marching between heavily armed police lines. Only Yoruba and another comrade were caught. I guess Yoruba as our minister of information had been pissing them off for a long time. Although they were taken into custody, the charges were immediately dismissed by the judge.

Then came the usual back and forth of negotiations. More incidents were to take place, but of a different sort now.

People who enter medical school surely find out what it means to have one of those professions where the temptation between serving free health clinics and buying a new BMW is strong. There are many doctors who disgrace themselves by becoming the eager slaves of money, high positions, privileges, and bourgeois attitudes. Instead of having self-respect as workers and protectors of the health of the people, they use their much-needed services to become supporters of a well-protected and self-regulated elite profession. The contradiction between those who supported medicine for the people, as well as preventive and multicultural homeopathic medicine, and those who preferred to embrace the class benefits of being a doctor, divided the medical community.

Many other problems and situations—some of them of quite a different origin—galvanized the situation. Fifteen days after the takeover, the Director of Pediatrics, Dr. Arnold Einhorn, reported that at least a dozen doctors of his team were threatening to resign because they claimed they had been subjected to harassment and intimidation by the Young Lords and other groups. They were the elitists who saw no value in what the patients and community thought was good for the hospital. The harassment and intimidation came, they said, from the "inflammatory statements" made by the Lords and "the presence of unauthorized persons" in the hospital. The "unauthorized persons" they were referring to, were the members of the Young Lords, the Think Lincoln Committee, and the Health Revolutionary Unity Movement running the complaints table at the hospital. The members of the groups also worked with patients as interpreters and helped hospital staff members fill out forms.

We were affronted that our eagerness and enthusiasm to help people in need was being construed by these doctors as a form of harassment. This was before the advent of patients' rights, and the majority of doctors treating low-income residents did not recognize health as a right but regarded it as a privilege. The attitude of the doctors who threatened to resign exemplified this for us. We were trying to replace that demeaning system with one based on respect for human dignity.

Dr. Lacot had an urgent meeting with fifty members of his staff and the medical board and the crisis was solved. We would continue doing our voluntary work and the doctors would not resign. We won most of them over to our side as we had with the patients, community, and health workers. At the end, the statement issued expressed that all of us, militants and faculty, wanted the same thing: better care for the patients. It was a resounding political victory for the Young Lords. We had set an example of the kind of things that can be accomplished when real cooperation is established between a hospital and the community it serves. That first round, however, would not be the last.

The struggle entered a new phase when Mayor Lindsay entered the fray. In the first week of August the news media was called to attend an event regarding a new development in the Lincoln Hospital issue. This time, the call was not made by us, but by City Hall. When reporters arrived at the nine-acre plot, bounded by Park and Morris Avenues and 144th and 149th Streets, they found a surrealistic image. A platform had been erected amid garbage and rubble on part of the designated land near East 148th Street. Community leaders, officials, politicians, medical doctors, and other people were gathering for the ceremony. At last, the land would be cleared for the construction of the new medical and mental-health center to replace the "old" Lincoln Hospital.

At the ceremony, the president of the newly created Health and Hospitals Corporation, Dr. Joseph T. English, stated, "Nowhere in the world have I seen health care delivered under such difficult circumstances." It was a very strong statement, acknowledging the abusive neglect to which the Bronx community had been subjected to by the government.

Dr. Lacot, who gained more moral stature in the eyes of the community with each day of this struggle, did not hesitate to address the city's new promises in his speech. "I cannot help thinking," he said, "of the many times that ceremonies of this sort are followed by long, agonizing periods of inactivity. I feel deeply concerned about the pace that future activities here will take. Therefore I demand, on behalf of this community to which I have committed myself to serve, that all of us at this podium who may in one way or another be instrumental in the process of building this hospital, leave no stone unturned to make sure that we will admit our first patients not later than the spring of 1974." This was another victory for the people.

The sequence of victories was too much for the powers that be. Besides the growing popularity of our struggle among different communities, each target grew more strategically important with subsequent offensives. Garbage was one thing—nobody wants to deal with it anyway—or seizing a community church—but taking on the city and the medical community was a direct hit. As our victories grew in importance, so did the ferocity of the counterattack.

There was another reason for the growing concern in government about the Young Lords. We were operating in many locations at the same time. While the Lincoln Hospital Offensive was being organized and carried out, a detachment of Young Lords were protecting youths who were being abused by the police in another part of the Bronx. At the same time, in Newark, our comrades were bravely fighting the New Jersey police at a Puerto Rican parade, and in Manhattan were humiliating pro-statehood governor Luis A. Ferré during the Puerto Rican Day Parade. Even more humiliating to our enemies' point of view, was that a producer had selected the Young Lords as one of the organizations that was to receive a large donation from revenue generated by ticket sales for a rock concert at Roosevelt Island featuring Funkadelic. Official resentment toward us was growing.

Then, just as things were beginning to look up at the hospital, another crisis erupted. The Young Lords heard from progressive doctors that charges were going to be presented against the director of Obstetrics and Gynecology. We questioned Carmen Rodriguez's botched legal abortion, which resulted in her death. We remembered that Puerto Rican women had been the guinea pigs for the birth control pharmaceutical-industrial complex, resulting in mass sterilization. We immediately questioned the practices and credentials of the staff. We wanted the director fired—and we succeeded, although the charges were disputed and the controversy led to the the temporary closing of the obstetric and gynecologic services of the hospital.

Because of this, Mayor Lindsay decided to move against the Young Lords and, with the strong backing of *The New York Times*, went to court and obtained an injunction barring us from "interfering" with the hospital. We backed off from having any authority or jurisdiction on who was hired or fired in the hospital, but our presence at the hospital continued. We continued to gain credibility within the community and Lincoln Hospital, although the offensive had faded away.

As in previous post-offensive periods, our ranks swelled with new recruits, especially healthcare workers. Our victories continued to attract college dropouts, unemployed youth, and other disenfranchised members of our community.

This time was also marked by a crisis in leadership within the Central Committee. I was in the process of exiting from the party and establishing the underground during this time, so I wasn't directly involved in the decision-making process anymore. Although majority ruled, the Central Committee was all-male, and most of the time ruled by consensus. In August 1970, Felipe was demoted from his position as chairman and spokesperson on the Central Committee for male chauvinist behavior. He was unfaithful to his wife, Iris Morales, a member of the central staff (the second level of leadership) of the organization. Iris and Felipe were complementary opposites, husband and wife in a monogamous relationship. Felipe had violated this bond and trust between them. Iris was furious and had the support of every woman in the organization.

The party continued the day-to-day work of organizing and overseeing our "Serve the People" programs (the general name for the free breakfast, clothes, and health programs), but we all were waiting to see if in fact we were all going to be measured by the same set of standards. Many of the men in the party viewed Felipe's transgression as a private issue between them. The women, particularly Iris, were adamant that this was an organizational, political concern. They forced these questions to be asked: "Are we in practice, not just in theory, what we profess to be? Are we serious about changing from within to create the outward revolution? Do we want to become women and men of the future?" Our organization was founded on the principles of complete openness about our lives and a firm commitment to respect our partners for life. We all had made commitments to each other under the rules of discipline of the party. Felipe's indiscretion was perceived as a serious infraction. He was sent back to the ranks as a non–ranking cadre for re-education. Although at the beginning he made a public statement expressing his agreement with the decision, later on Felipe left the Young Lords; he never made it to "the Second People's Church."

Felipe's departure had two effects: Publicly, we had lost the most recognized person and voice of the Young Lords. Privately, we had lost our charismatic leader. His exit challenged the organization's leadership to reassess their methods, and cadres had to overcome hero worship and personal loyalties in order to continue to be part of the forward motion of the organization. I was already underground and had little contact with Felipe but I still felt a deep loss. However, I was under party discipline, and agreed with the decision of the Central Committee. Felipe was the first Young Lord I had recruited, and he trusted me. I had lost someone very important to me, someone who was always beside me, ready to take a blow and fight like hell for what we believed in. The organization survived Felipe's exit mainly because the party had been founded on a set of principles and politics that transcended any individual, but his loss was one I certainly felt.

The struggle continued. On November 10, 1970, four months after the initial takeover, we were back in action at Lincoln Hospital. Just when many people were not expecting a new Young Lords offensive there, the doctors and nurses received a surprise "visit" from community people, many of them addicted to heroin. Using surprise as the main tactic, we took over the residents' auditorium and announced that we had decided to run a drug detoxification program right there. Thus the Lincoln Detox Program was born. Before the astonished eyes of many personnel, we began organizing the space and setting up as casually as someone might change the furniture at home. During that offensive I met Vicente "Panamá" Alba, he was sent by H.RUM to participate in the takeover. He, like my high school buddy Charlie, had been adopted as a Puerto Rican—in this case, a "PanaRican." It was also at Lincoln Hospital that I met Jennifer Dohrn. Her sister, Bernadine, was with the Weather Underground. Jennifer joined our staff and we dated and lived together.

We had again addressed an issue important to the community. During those days there was a lot of concern in New York, as well as other cities, regarding a dramatic increase in the consumption of heroin that was being described as an epidemic. One out of every five people in the Mott Haven area of the Bronx was addicted. The whole borough of the Bronx lacked a detox-ification program, inpatient or out. Once again, we had exposed a particular case of oppression through a lack of services and demonstrated a way to creatively address the issue.

Another aspect of the new offensive was that this time around, the support from people working in the hospital was so decisive that the police were unable to even consider removing anyone by force. Several doctors belonging to the Doctors/Pediatrics Collective and who had taken part in the first takeover, joined us this time as well. The department of psychiatry at the hospital provided methadone under Dr. Steve Levine's license, and we began to detoxify heroin addicts in ten-day cycles.

Awakening people's social conscience was essential to our detox effort. We used political education classes as our therapeutic tool to rehabilitate drug addicts. This was something that even many of the health professionals who contacted us were not familiar with. We used the theory of Black Panther Michael Tabor, who went underground. He had developed a pamphlet entitled "Capitalism + Dope = Genocide." The practical lesson was simple; it opened up your mind to endless possibilities. People without hope feel they have no options when faced with a choice between life and death. We wanted to provide motivation for personal improvement within a political context so that we could all work together and fight back to end this destructive cycle. We also wanted to provide a detox alternative to methadone. The political context of heroin resulted in mass substance abuse, and we had to find a way out. We studied the experiences of the Chinese when they were faced with opium addiction after their revolution. Joshua Horn, a British physician who was in China for twenty years, published *Away with All Pests*, wherein he described in great detail the role of acupuncture in open heart surgery, reattachment of limbs, and in drug rehabilitation. For the first time on the East Coast, acupuncture was used to treat the secondary effects of heroin once the addict was "clean." In order to have enough personnel to provide treatment for the addicts, we established the first acupuncture training program on the Atlantic seaboard. I had the personal satisfaction of seeing my childhood friend Walter Bosque become the first Latino acupuncturist on the East Coast.

Many of the rehabilitated drug addicts remained in the program as volunteers, an apprenticeship leading to employment. Some actually became members of the Young Lords or joined different community groups. It was a great joy to witness people who had been suffering from addiction, so often despised and dismissed by society as lost causes, rehabilitated and transformed into community leaders.

The program was such a success that the city government had no choice but to provide funding. That money was received in July of 1971, nine months later. Until then, a lot of people worked for free and we treated between six hundred and eight hundred patients a week. By 1979 the program was so successful that thirteen employees in leadership positions at Lincoln Detox, including me and Panamá, were transferred to seven municipal hospitals throughout the city. Although we fought the move for months, the city successfully broke up the cohesive leadership at "the people's drug program." Since then, the Lincoln Detoxification Program has been recognized by the U.N. for their innovative work in the area of substance abuse and recovery. What began as a fringe treatment has become mainstream. For over thirty years Lincoln has been providing recovery services to the people of New York City. This is the one and only institution we built, and it remains as an important legacy.

THE SECOND PEOPLE'S CHURCH

LESS THAN TWO YEARS after the Young Lords' home debut via the Garbage Offensive, we were being targeted by a government counterintelligence program (Cointelpro) bent on destroying the organization as it had done to so many others. They operated primarily through infiltration and sabotage, and their methods were at times violent. More than thirty years after the murder of Julio Roldán, the case remains unsolved; details of the murder designed to fracture our group are still unknown, as are the identities of the assassins and their leaders. Not until all of the files surrounding his death are declassified will we ever know what really happened. I do know one thing for sure: his death was a turning point in the organization and was pivotal in bringing about our disintegration.

Julio was a Vietnam veteran, one of those forgotten heroes who came back home to find ingratitude and even hostility from the same system that had ordered him to risk his life and kill. He was an open book. His kindness, generosity, and commitment were limitless. I cannot think about him without smiling. What a great cook he was! In charge of the kitchen at our headquarters, Julio masterfully prepared typical Puerto Rican food for all of the Young Lords. No four-star Latino restaurant anywhere could do it better. If the old Latino proverb is true, that "love enters through the kitchen," then there could be no doubt that every Young Lord had a very special appreciation for Julio. In fact, the "ideological" impact of Julio's cooking was so significant, that, no one ever missed a meal with Julio at the community men's hall. There were instances when journalists, unaware of our "barrio gourmet" cooking, believed that we were exaggerating when we raved about our "home-cooked" meals.

Cooking wasn't Julio's only important asset. At age thirty-four, the war veteran was also highly skilled with weapons, and an example of exquisite combat discipline. For those reasons, among others, he was regarded as one of our best cadres. The ones responsible for his murder had chosen their prey with utmost precision; Julio's premature departure affected each and every one of us in the Young Lords for many long months. We were all perfectly aware of the vicious nature in which he had been eliminated from our lives.

It happened this way:

Despite our success gaining the support of the people of El Barrio regarding public sanitation, every now and then City Hall would forget to pick up the garbage in El Barrio. It was a frustrating problem for our people. Yet every time the garbage in our neighborhood was ignored, the people would simply fight back by applying the same tactics: More garbage would be piled up and burned in the street to force firefighters and other city authorities to pay attention to this problem. The burning of garbage became a natural response whenever El Barrio was overwhelmed by extra *basura*. This went on for a while, until the bureaucrats decided we were causing serious difficulties and sent trucks regularly to pick up our garbage at the same rate as in the rich neighborhoods.

In mid-September 1970, we were conducting one of those phenomenal Garbage Offensives when the police decided to make a move on us. As Julio and Bobby Lemus were standing on a street corner, a policeman walked toward them and screamed, "You're under arrest!" They were immediately handcuffed and accused of arson. According to the official charges, they had tried to start a fire in one of El Barrio's tenement buildings in the past. Naturally, no one with any common sense believed that a model member of the Young Lords would set fire to a building where Puerto Rican families lived. Julio's arrest was shocking and extremely peculiar—a surprise for those who knew him. Julio and Bobby were sent to the infamous "Tombs," a jail complex in downtown Manhattan. In order to set them free we needed to put up a bail of $1,500 for each one. There was no way for us to raise that kind of money quickly. None of us knew how critical it would be for us to act immediately. We never could have imagined what happened next.

The next morning, prison authorities announced that Julio was found hanging by the neck in his solitary-confinement cell. They made sure to call his death a "suicide." Anyone close to him knew he was incapable of taking his own life. Absolutely convinced of that, the Young Lords sent a pathologist to attend the official autopsy. As expected, there was evidence of foul play. Some of Julio's bones were broken and his body showed other signs of a beating.

His violent death was not the only bizarre "suicide" of an imprisoned "minority" member during those days. A subsequent investigation revealed that at least eight other inmates had "committed suicide" in exactly the same manner as Julio. Strangely, this specific case—despite the outrage expressed among the Latino community in New York—was poorly investigated by Mayor Lindsay's administration. A few months later, an "official report" conducted by a group selected by City Hall—including Geraldo Rivera, William J. van den Heuvel, chairman of the New York City Board of Corrections, Rose M. Singer, Nyrka Torrando Alum, and David Schulte—"reconfirmed" the police's claim. The report was a whitewash, a farce. I wasn't alone in my thinking. Julio's murder triggered an immediate and dramatic response from the Young Lords. I had disappeared from view temporarily, but Julio's murder brought me back.

At once, we decided to take over the Methodist church again. This time, for the first time, we would brandish weapons. They were meant to be symbolic; we wanted to force the city to negotiate with us for prison reforms. We were angry and wanted to show how serious we were, publicly and on TV. But before the final decision was made, Juan came to see me privately with a political and military concern. He wanted my political opinion about the viability of the operation since I was the highest-ranking military person in the party. I fully agreed with the plans set forth by the Central Committee. In addition, he wanted to make sure that I could supply the aboveground organization with weapons and ammunition. Time was short—we had only two days to prepare—but I knew we could do it.

On the afternoon of October 18, a Young Lords detachment went to the funeral home where Julio's body was lying, and took possession of the coffin. They draped it in a huge Puerto Rican flag and carried it on their shoulders through the streets, toward the church. This time we had prepared our community, so that we could stand united, as one defiant people. Our party had sent out the call to different radical groups around the country for support, including the Black Panther Party, El Comité MINP, El Movimiemento Pro-Independencia, I Wor Kun, Youth Against War and Fascism, and a few others. We made sure to make a special call to our community, the people of El Barrio, to join us in a celebration of Julio's life. The response was over-whelming. No one had ever seen a bigger crowd in the streets of El Barrio.

Inside the coffin, along with the body, was a surprise designed to send a message to the police about repercussions for threat-ening the Young Lords and the barrio community. As a seasoned soldier, Julio was performing his last deed. The coffin swayed from side to side with the extra weight.

Early that night the enormous procession arrived at the church. The Young Lords broke in, set the coffin on the altar, opened it, and removed the guns that were inside. Armed guards were positioned at each end of the coffin. Immediately we held a press conference. Yoruba announced that the Lords' policy of not using weapons had ended, and that "from here on, we are ready to defend ourselves and the community 'by whichever manner.' " There was no going back now. Journalists watched in shock as we stood guard around the casket displaying shotguns, pistols, and carbines. The next day, newspapers carried the story, highlighted by the picture of our armed honor guard with the coffin at the Spanish Methodist Church, which had already been rebaptized for the second time as "the People's Church."

Now the city government was facing a new dilemma. The Young Lords had been prompted to a more militant action in response to the assassination of one of our cadres. Public support was huge. We had displayed a tactic that made it virtually impossible for the police to provoke us, while at the same time the government could not be sure to what lengths we were willing to go.

A new minister had taken charge of the parish, a Puerto Rican who immediately expressed his endorsement of our idea for the church, but not our method. Despite New York City Mayor John Lindsay's statement that the takeover of a church "is a sacrilege," the new minister wouldn't request police intervention. This was the only thing that prevented the police from storming the building. Since we made sure no one had "seen" the delivery of the weapons, the police couldn't issue a weapons violation charge. We were aware of our constitutional right. We had created a political situation that placed the church between us and the authorities. With that information, we knew the authorities had their hands tied. Furthermore, we had decided not to allow the police inside the church.

Still, a couple of cops tried to venture inside the building, where the Young Lords were busy putting together our social program for the community as we had done during the first takeover. We stopped them. "You're not welcome here," they were told. One of the policemen ignored the warning and kept walking in. He was confronted at once by Felix Vazquez, another Vietnam veteran, who was in charge of the entrance to the church. "Officers," he said firmly, "you are not permitted to enter this church." Felix acted with obvious determination. Sensing that perhaps the Puerto Rican youngsters with the carbines were actually bluffing, the policeman who had been doing the talking made a move to force his entry. "Cock your weapons!" Felix yelled. The other guards obeyed him without hesitation. The policemen froze. How long would the standoff last? The picture was immobile for a few seconds—less than five—but it was the type of moment that seems to last an eternity, and from which community legends are created.

The policemen performed an about-face and fled the premises.

The community knew Felix quite well. We knew him better. Many of us had witnessed the time when a hysterical mother had rushed into our Bronx office screaming that her child had stopped breathing. Without hesitation Felix rushed to the building to find a baby, unable to breathe, lying on one of the upper floors. Felix immediately started mouth-to-mouth resuscitation while running downstairs, holding the baby against his chest. He redoubled his already exhausting attempt by making an effort to control the air pressure he was sending into the fragile lungs of the baby, and he never slowed down to regain his own strength. The crowd cheered with surprise when Felix appeared at the front doors of the building, to hand the baby to the paramedics. Right then and there we all saw Felix fall unconscious to the ground.

That was our Felix. He was not brave only when he was holding a shotgun; he was brave, period. Men and women like him were the ones who made the Young Lords a success. We performed random acts of kindness and cooperation on a daily basis.

The liberal city government understood the determination of every Young Lord in the church. City Hall knew that we would not back off from a confrontation. They suspected there would be serious problems if they tried to get us out by force. And the truth was that the underground had retaliatory plans in the event the cops did storm the church.

However, New York's Finest would not surrender so easily. Now it seemed that the church experience had become a face-saving issue for them. Our purpose was not to aimlessly humiliate the cops. What we wanted was to show a way to encourage community pride, self-determination, and self-defense.

Later, two other cops appeared. This time they used another approach. They requested permission to enter the building in a polite manner. Yoruba told them it was okay and that they could carry their official handguns, but that they had to be checked for concealed weapons. The two submitted themselves to a body search while the crowd cheered and Yoruba told them, smiling, that we wanted to make sure no one would plant anything inside the church. Of course, after conducting a very brief inspection inside the church, the two cops came out and assured the press that they had found nothing illegal or out of order.

The next day, the newspapers further humiliated the police. One headline read: "Policemen Frisked by the Young Lords."

In the meantime, the pastor of the church had agreed to form a Cleric Committee and request access to the Tombs to conduct an independent investigation into the so-called "suicides." The mayor rejected the proposal. Nevertheless, such action provided us with a credibility uncommon at the time. In addition, we now had the backing of church representatives. This status reached a peak with the visit to New York of the Puerto Rican Catholic bishop Antulio Parrilla, who conducted a religious ceremony in the church for those "assassinated" in the Riker's Island detention facility. We were standing firm regarding the public-opinion battle, as the political bureaucrats in City Hall struggled to move out of their corner.

Aware of the mood in the city, we made another move—we offered to purchase the church. Not surprisingly, the offer was rejected. The church's superintendent, Dr. Osborne, was not a sympathizer, which helped to further increase the mobilization of the community. Unfortunately, the response was more repression, and some Young Lords were arrested for such offenses as "raising money publicly to buy a church."

All this represented another change. The gravitational center of these actions was shifting from strictly community issues like garbage collection and day-care centers, to abuses against inmates in the prisons system, and Puerto Rico's independence.

When the coffin with the remains of Julio was placed in the sanctuary for the honor guard on the first day of the takeover, one of the flags displayed was that of the Nationalist Party of Puerto Rico. That organization figured prominently in the list of the various groups that were subjected to surveillance, disruption, and harassment by the FBI's Cointelpro agenda. We were placing ourselves within firing range of one of the most implacable secret police operations in America. We were subsequently placed on the priority lists of the agencies in charge of persecuting political and military activists. All of a sudden, a Puerto Rican patriot had become a dangerous species as far as the United States Justice Department was concerned.

The Young Lords were in the process of learning more and more through experience, as we enjoyed our succession of victories. The stories about our "Offensive postures" were making the news almost daily. The press was also reporting stories about different aspects of our revolutionary life. The public was provided with interesting features about the women in the Young Lords Party, the political side of our quests, the insights, analysis, and the constant commentaries favoring our political agenda.

The police forces, however, were closing in and obviously looking for excuses to nail us. We took that as a warning shot. We had to be aware. There were instances in which the perpetrator in any arrest made by the police in El Barrio would automatically be identified as a Young Lord. The police were looking to damage our reputation by trying to illustrate us as common criminals.

Early in December, a judge issued an order to force our eviction from the church. That was the moment the police were waiting for. If we resisted the court order, they could raid the building, with or without the pastor's consent, and if we abandoned the building carrying weapons, we could all be arrested.

When the moment came to leave the building, the policemen were astonished to discover that there were no weapons . . . not even a trace. The Young Lords came out of the church completely "clean." The policemen had missed the couriers carrying the weapons out of the building. Our beloved neighborhood *doñas* had carried parts of the disassembled guns out of the church in their shopping bags, right under the policemen's noses! It was another job well done. True, by the time the guns made it back to the underground, many of the parts did not match and most of the guns could never be put back together again. Disappointing, yes, but it was more important that the operation had brought together the Young Lord's, the community, and the underground.

In the underground, the recruitment effort was taking a definitive shape. We recruited based on a pyramid structure, the foundation being my most trusted childhood friends. That prevented enemy infiltration and would eventually lead us to operate a cell in Puerto Rico.

The aftermath of this successful offensive again resulted in an increase in new recruits. After the Second People's Church Offensive, the Young Lords Party transformed itself into a comparatively large paramilitary political organization practically owned by the Puerto Rican people. By then we had established several branches throughout the northeast. The new path we had decided to take would lead to still more profound changes in our organization and community.

THE RISE AND FALL OF THE
YOUNG LORDS PARTY

THE YOUNG LORDS ORIGINALLY ATTRACTED A large following because the organization quickly developed the capacity to respond to our needs as a community and as individuals. The community needs had been brought to the forefront during the East Harlem riots of 1967. Individually, we were a generation of people without a history, alienated from our culture, and without a national identity. The Young Lords was the organization that struggled to link a disconnected generation to our past.

The struggle was both internal and external. The external struggle was easier to understand. The issues in our communities were obvious: police violence, poor housing, full and equal employment, education, health care. We challenged a system of inequity, a system that denigrated our culture, language, and capacity to organize and fight back. The internal struggle was more difficult to navigate because it required us to look inside ourselves, and to reflect honestly on how much we had internalized the prevailing political ideologies of racism, sexism, and individualism. To face that reality, challenge it, and change ourselves into men and women with a new value system that honored the equality of all of us, was more difficult.

The Young Lords became a vehicle through which we reaffirmed our newfound national identity. The Lords became a place where we each brought our individuality and wove it into the fabric of a collective process to link us to the past and to address our plight as a people. We were transformed from a dependent colonial people to a people capable of charting a path to social justice and independence. We publicly rejected the established norms and American values for the integration of our own cultural value system. We began to reject ideas that perpetuated the supremacy of the male, the dehumanization of homosexuals, and the inequality of our diverse racial origins. The Young Lords rapidly associated with and developed mass organizations that were issue-oriented to address specific needs of the Puerto Rican community. Our service programs included everything from free clothing drives to free legal services. The Puerto Rican Students Union (PRSU) evolved into the student front of the Young Lords organizing on college campuses and our communities. H.RUM became a citywide vehicle to confront the health crises in our community and to fight for the rights of health-care workers. We established the Lincoln Detox Program, and Obereros Unidos—the first effort to organize Puerto Rican factory workers. The Latin Women's Collective gave women the opportunity to address their unique concerns and to develop their own agenda.

The Young Lords were vocal advocates on behalf of prisoners' rights. When the Attica prison riot exploded on September 9, 1971, the inmates asked for two representatives from the Young Lords to be sent in to observe the negotiations. Fi and ex-Viceroy and Young Lord Jose "G.I." Pari represented us in the talks. The Young Lords kept alive the legacy of the heroic men of the Sixty-fifth Infantry, an all–Puerto Rican unit that was decimated during the Korean War, by naming our veterans' organization "the Sixty-fifth." The clandestine organization that I directed was to plan to respond militarily to any aggression against the party or the people.

Despite all of this activity and drive, after the summer of 1971 the Young Lords were in decline. A number of factors had contributed to this, but for me most relevant were those that illustrated the growing separation between the Young Lords and the constituents of our community, *el pueblo*.

There were a growing number of Puerto Ricans attending colleges and universities in the United States. We were undoubtedly beneficiaries of the civil-rights and Black Power movements of the late 1960s. Within that community, the achievements of the black liberation movement and militant sector of the anti-war movement inspired many. Our successful takeover of the First People's Church inspired other members of the Puerto Rican community to confront institutions of power. Militant students began to organize themselves around revolutionary student platforms, and to promote direct-action on campuses.

The growth of the student movement was inevitable; they lived in our communities, and the early leadership of the Lords was rooted in the nascent stages of the Puerto Rican student movement. Many of us knew each other; we were counterparts— they were on campuses and we were in the streets. Every so often we would find ourselves on the streets together.

The PRSU was developed to address the need for open admissions and free tuition in public higher education. Their list of demands included the establishment of Black and Puerto Rican Studies departments at the universities, as well as an end to police violence, and providing affordable housing and community health rights for those in the barrios. As their activism progressed, more students began to focus their attention on the political and economic situation of their homeland, Puerto Rico. *Machete* was published as the official newspaper of PRSU and had wide distribution on college campuses in the Northeast.

The result of the educational and organizing efforts by the PRSU led to a massive and spirited conference at Columbia University in September of 1970, sponsored jointly with the Young Lords. The theme was the liberation of Puerto Rico, and hundreds of high-school and college students attended. The conference helped us to organize a "Free Puerto Rico Now" committee, throughout high-school and college campuses, as well as kick off another massive event we had planned for the following month, even with the second takeover of the People's Church in full swing. On October 30, 1970—the twentieth anniversary of the day in 1950 that the Nationalist Party started a rebellion in Puerto Rico—over ten thousand people marched to the United Nations from El Barrio, calling for independence, freedom for all political prisoners, including five Puerto Rican Nationalist prisoners (at the time, the longest-held political prisoners in the western hemisphere) and an end to police violence in our communities. This was, to date, the largest anti-colonial street demonstration set up by mainland Puerto Ricans.

This was the most intense period of Puerto Rican student activism, leaving a legacy of ethnic studies departments at every CUNY campus and the establishment of the only bilingual college on the East Coast—Maria Eugenio de Hostos Community

College—in the South Bronx, the largest Puerto Rican community outside of the island of Puerto Rico.

Following the success of the "Free Puerto Rico Now" conference at Columbia University in September of 1970, and the impact of the mass mobilization at the U.N. that fall, a political struggle developed within the leadership of the Young Lords. The Central Committee was divided on the role of mainland Puerto Ricans in the struggle for the national liberation of Puerto Rico, and the role of Puerto Rican workers in the multinational working class struggle within the U.S. What was once a unified leadership began to polarize. The revolutionary nationalist contingent of the party won this tug-of-war, and the result was the decision to open up branches of the Young Lords in Puerto Rico. In March of 1971 the Young Lords Party launched the "Ofenciva Rompe Cadenas" (Break the Chains) on the anniversary of the Ponce Massacre.

The plan was as ambitious as it was foolish. First-generation Puerto Ricans, born, raised and educated in the U.S., mainly from Northeastern urban cities, were going to export revolution to Puerto Rico. We put our resources and ourselves at risk, and had grossly misunderstood the political situation on the island. We published a bilingual edition of *Pa'lante* and shipped it to Puerto Rico. It proved to be irrelevant. We should have asked ourselves why they would need our brand of nationalism in light of their already established, and strong, nationalist tradition. The move didn't do much to help Puerto Ricans, but it hurt us on the mainland by reducing the number of experienced cadres and leaders who were available to carry out the day-to-day work of the Young Lords in the States. A branch in Puerto Rico defected from the main organization. People began to leave; community offices closed all over the city.

Then we made a decision that would prove fatal to the organization. The New York City Puerto Rican Day Parade had evolved into a national gathering of Puerto Ricans from around the country as well as Puerto Rico. We felt it was commercializing our culture and our pride. In 1970 we protested the grand marshal, Puerto Rico's Miss Universe Malisol Malaret, as an affront to revolutionary Latina women. In 1971, in response to growing police violence, the Young Lords decided to prevent the police from marching first in the parade, their traditional spot in all New York City parades. We trained defense cadres from all our branches in order to take over the front of the parade. Our intention was an open secret. Essentially we challenged the cops for control of the parade.

The day arrived and everyone had their orders to meet at 57th Street and Fifth Avenue at eight A.M. I recently had surgery and was post-operative and "politically inactive." My responsibilities included reconnaissance, intelligence, and evaluation. Everyone was armed with the standard Young Lords weapons of engagement—llawawa sticks, nunchakus, Chinese stars, and oversize marbles—in anticipation of the mounted police. The front line had been assured by defense leadership that football helmets would be distributed at the parade site, but they never received them.

Our adventurous plan allowed the police to anticipate our moves and swiftly attack us from every direction. Those moments are forever frozen in my mind. The sound of breaking glass grew louder than the drum and bugle corps warming up in the side streets. As I turned toward the cries of people trying to get out of the way, I saw horses charging ordinary people. They pursued them into the park, beat people at random, and trampled on others. The police attacked indiscriminately throughout the parade route. The organized units of cadres had been scattered, and everyone was chaotically trying to get out of the area. Everyone witnessed the horror of it all. Never mind that we'd put ourselves in danger—we'd also jeopardized the safety of the thousands of people that we'd vowed to "serve and protect." Throughout the afternoon and into the evening, members would call headquarters for information on the day's casualties.

The biggest fatality that day was the trust we had gained from the people. The reaction was immediate. The following morning, people who would normally stop by our offices on their way to work, crossed the street in order to avoid us. The people that came to our offices on a daily basis, dramatically decreased. The *doñas* who had kept us well fed on home cooking didn't care anymore if we had eaten or not. The organization had suffered our first public political and military defeat, and it hit us hard. This fueled the growing discontent among the cadres, the foundation of the party.

Leadership could no longer ignore the fact that going to Puerto Rico had been a monumental mistake. Members of the Central Committee were assigned the task of going to Puerto Rico, taking over the leadership and resolving that branch of the organization's issues. The Central Committee recommended that we retreat back to the U.S. In mid-1971, after the retreat was complete, disciplinary reassignments of members resulted in a new Central Committee and a new leadership that centered around Gloria Gonzalez Frontanez. Under her, the political direction of the Young Lords shifted and its goals reoriented toward building a Maoist political party in the U.S., bent on fomenting revolution among workers. The party was renamed the Puerto Rican Revolutionary Workers Organization. Everyone was sent into factories to organize the proletariat, and the struggle for social justice for mainland Puerto Ricans became increasingly irrelevant.

My life was coming apart. The organization I had once helped to organize had become disconnected from the people in our communities. I called a meeting of the underground leadership of the military to discuss the new political direction of the party. After thirty-six hours we produced a paper entitled, "Thirty-six Hour Offensive," outlining our concerns with the new emphasis of the party and the abandonment of the service programs that had made us popular in and beyond our communities.

My ideological struggle with Juan, representing the new Central Committee, proved to be words to the wind. Worthless now, we were all expected to abandon the clandestine work and become cadres in the newly formed organization. I flashed back to those days in front of Loeb at Columbia, where I first met Juan. We had been through a number of successful campaigns together; we had a special relationship that was to be severed for years. We had formed a clandestine organization and had the capacity to synchronize and coordinate action in the northeast United States and in Puerto Rico. Members of the underground had sacrificed much. I felt I had the lives of many in the balance of my decisions. It was the most difficult political decision I had to make. I told Juan that the cadres and the underground were adamant about continuing our service and assistance programs within our communities. To eliminate them at the expense of some ultra-left deviation to solely concentrate on the Puerto Rican working-class would end the Young Lords tradition—teaching by example and taking to the streets. As I spoke to Juan, I felt I was being insubordinate to a higher-ranking political comrade. I knew in my bones that we were politically correct and that Puerto Rican Revolutionary Workers Organization had committed a serious error in political judgment. I returned to my leadership collective and shared with them the painful truth.

We had no choice but to issue orders to all underground members to abandon their structures, destroy what they can't hide and begin to distance themselves from each other until it was clear that the dismantling of the underground had not been detected by the state. Months later, our people in Puerto Rico received the same order. What I had dedicated my life to was evaporating like mist from a teapot. A myriad of insecurities simmered to the surface; how could we serve the people without the Young Lords?

Some Lords remained in the new organization and became immersed in strenuous Maoist study groups and ideological struggles that replaced garbage offensives and breakfast programs. I couldn't stomach the transition. Because of the social and political isolation of the new group, cultlike characteristics emerged. Deviation from the party line was not tolerated, and those who did speak up were subject to psychological torture, kidnappings, and beatings. The kidnapping and beating of Richie Perez and Diana Caballero in particular brought many of us together to publicly denounce the increasing violence of the organization. Yoruba and Iris were also detained against their will. It appeared to many of us that the government-sponsored Cointelpro had taken root in our movement. Through infiltration, agents of this national security program had destroyed many civil-rights organizations, and, in some cases, as in the Black Panther Party, arranged the death of members.

We were young, determined, and uncompromising in our desire to build a better world. Every Young Lord lives with the pride their contribution made to the historical process. We also live with the failures and shortcomings. Inexperienced, we took on the most advanced empire of modern times and in our youthful eagerness were outmaneuvered in the end. Cointelpro can claim success in disrupting the Puerto Rican liberation movement in the United States. We knew they were there; it is not clear how many agents actually made it into positions of leadership in the party. To think otherwise is to *"taperl el cielo con una mano"* (cover the sky with a hand). We don't know how many of our failures were government-directed. What is clear is that there were no agents in our underground. What is equally clear is that all the evidence indicates that, with its final breath, the Lords' leadership directed the kidnappings and beatings. As Lords, we lived with the premise that "practice is the criterion for truth." The practices of those who led us on the path to self-destruction are suspicious, and many of us hold those members responsible. If they weren't agents, they should have collected a paycheck for their role in the destruction. Most important, history will hold us all accountable.

THE SEIZURE OF THE STATUE OF LIBERTY

BY 1977 THE POLITICAL PHENOMENON once called the Young Lords had withered away, but there were some of us who kept the fire alive in our hearts. The organization had made important contributions for the betterment of our people, although the abuses toward our communities continued and so did colonialism in Puerto Rico. Some of the former Young Lords still felt the urge to combat these injustices.

After the implosion of the Young Lords, some of us—who just a few years before had been showing off with great pride our purple berets—were making great efforts to hide our past. In some cases, concealment was a way to silence bad memories and in others it was the only way to get on with "normal" life in society. Jennifer and I had two children. Amilcar (named after

Amilcar Cabral, revolutionary leader of Guinea-Bissau) was born on August 19, 1974 and Haydee (named after Cuban revolutionary Haydee Santamaria) on April 16, 1976. Many were just trying to survive economically while others struggled with a very deep sense of bitterness and abandonment. The experience was over too soon. Like a heartbroken lover pining for a lost beloved, it was difficult to go on.

I had dedicated so much of my time and energy to direct political action on issues that affected our (Puerto Rican) community, I decided to do what I knew how to do best—organize a direct action that would bring national attention to our five political prisoners. I called on Panamá, and a group of people including ex–Young Lords like Richie Perez and Diana Caballero, from the Committee to Free the Nationalist Puerto Rican Political Prisoners, to discuss a plan. Before long, twenty-eight comrades joined the effort. Most of them were Puerto Ricans, but there were also gringos, Japanese, Cubans, and African-Americans. Many of the people who came were members of different groups, like the Puerto Rican Solidarity Committee and the Union of Patriotic Puerto Ricans. We each had different ideas of what we should do, but I was adamant that it had to be something that would produce solid results. That was part of our training as Young Lords. The answers I was looking for were in my memories of those earlier days.

I was proud to be a founding member of the Young Lords Party, a group that was able to get conspicuous and positive results. My commitment to the Young Lords was not in vain. We had accomplished breakthroughs, both real and symbolic. We developed confidence in people from the barrios by showing that to fight for one's basic rights is to be dignified. We believed that a righteous fight is always worth the effort, no matter the physical or political power of the opposition.

That attitude helped us play a critical role in the struggle to improve services in our communities. We contributed to a political reality that reflected a new and progressive consciousness among Puerto Ricans. This new landscape was the contextual background that provided the environment for Puerto Ricans to join the electoral process. For the first time, Puerto Ricans campaigned for public office and were elected in significant numbers. Unfortunately, we didn't understand the role of electoral politics as a tactic to achieve our overall strategy. Therefore, we created a vacuum that was filled, for the most part, by individuals sophisticated enough to cut a slice of the American "political pie" for themselves. Many were clearly not committed to the Puerto Rican community. The Young Lords became the first true symbol of community protection for the poor in the Puerto Rican ghettos of several states. We were trusted more than the government agencies. Local party chapters in the different pockets of our barrios received more complaints about delinquency, police abuse, and domestic abuse than the police precincts or Puerto Rican elected officials did. For the first time in their lives, Puerto Ricans stood up to social outcasts and bullies from the barrios. "If you mess with me, I'll call the Young Lords," was a common threat.

Now we had to translate all of that experience into a feasible plan considering our new circumstances and conditions. I was no longer as young as I had been, and the focus of most of the people and groups with which I was now connected had broader goals than those of the original Young Lords. I had to think of an action that would satisfy everyone and, most importantly, have a clear message and objective.

Oscar Collazo had been in jail since 1950 for the attack on Blair House, the temporary residence of President Harry S. Truman. Rafael Cancel Miranda, Irvin Flores, Andrés Figueroa Cordero, and the leader, Lolita Lebrón, were in for the attack on the U.S. Congress in 1954. We saw them as national heroes, while others in the United States viewed them as dangerous criminals. Their seemingly endless imprisonment—much longer than the sentences imposed on ruthless gangsters—was beginning to embarrass the U.S. justice system worldwide. Campaigns for their release, either because of humanitarian reasons or as a step toward the solution of the colonial relationship with Puerto Rico, were gaining momentum. The heat was reaching the new president, Jimmy Carter. The hypocrisy of his policy promoting human rights in Latin America and in the world while the Puerto Rican nationalists, the longest-held political prisoners in the western hemisphere, were kept behind bars, was apparent.

Several protest actions were taking place. At one point, four thousand people marched on the streets of Washington, D.C., in support of the release of the Puerto Rican nationalists. Labor unions, political organizations, and community groups backed the activity. Congressman Roberto Garcia, a Democrat from New York, had started to put pressure on the U.S. Department of Justice, demanding the unconditional release of the Puerto Rican nationalists. One critical person behind the congressman's efforts was his executive assistant, Marlene Cintrón, a former member of the Young Lords Party. Coincidently I met Marlene at Old Westbury. I was the student who interviewed her and recommended her admission to the newly formed college.

There was a lot of activity in various areas on the East Coast around this issue. I wanted an action-packed protest inspired by the specific issue of the Puerto Rican political prisoners. I thought of a daring coup: the appropriation of the Statue of Liberty. We would fly the Puerto Rican flag from its crown and demand the release of our heroes. It would send an unmistakable message to the American people and remind them how deceitful it was to say that the United States was committed to "liberty and justice for all" while Puerto Rico remained oppressed by U.S. corporations and armed forces, and while Puerto Rican freedom-fighters languished in U.S. jails.

The message was meant for Puerto Ricans, too: Be proud of our freedom fighters, defend them. Panamá, Richie Perez, and I presented the idea to the twenty-eight courageous men and women of the group. All of them were seasoned fighters, and there was one possible infiltrator. This multi-national group placed their trust and confidence in the leadership that was directing the action. The date was tentively set for the end of October, to commemorate the October 30, 1950, Nationalist uprising in the town of Jayuya, Puerto Rico.

We began to collect intelligence on the Statue of Liberty and its surroundings. It didn't take us long to learn about the security guards—how many and where they were stationed, what time they started and finished work, the exact hour they took time off to rest, or to eat. We learned the ferry schedules, and found out when the place was the most and the least crowded. We learned the location of every entrance and exit and window. We learned as many details as we could to prepare for any contingency.

The twenty-eight *compañeros* were divided into seven groups of four and directed to get to Battery Park by different routes. We acted as if we didn't know each other. At a given moment everyone was directed toward the Statue of Liberty ferry. I can remember that while boarding the vessel I took a deep breath and noticed the sky. It was a foggy New York morning but the sky was gray. Hopefully not too many people would decide to go to see the Lady in the Harbor today.

The ferry was not crowded with adults but there were about forty elementary-school children running around. I took mental

note of the schoolkids. That could present a problem. We became seriously concerned. The physical and emotional welfare
of the children was of prime importance and the whole plan
could be derailed. I was overcome by a sense of irony and the
thought that such an important action was on the verge of disruption by a bunch of innocent ten-year-olds. We had not
counted on such an obvious possibility—of children being present. Our intelligence had never reported class trips. All the steps
had been cautiously planned and rehearsed. We were confident
that we could close our eyes and do our assignment to perfec-
tion—and now this. My mind worked quickly. There was only
one option: The whole first phrase of the operation—securing
the statue—had to be done even faster than we had planned, to
prevent any clash with the children.

As soon as the ferry docked, the operation got under way.
Twenty-eight adults began to run like hell toward the statue. We
got there before the kids or the other people in the ferry. Out
of breath and gasping for air to speak to the oncoming tourists,
we blocked the main entrance. After taking control of the entrance, we told the people that no one was allowed into the
building. With the same authoritative tone, we ordered the federal employees, and other workers, to leave immediately. We told
them that if they refused, members of our group would carry
them out. They were so taken aback by the orders that nobody
made a move to resist. As soon as the last person left the building, all the entrances were closed and locked. In about fifteen
minutes, we had seized and secured the Statue of Liberty.

Once we were completely in charge, I telephoned Panamá,
who had stayed behind with Diana Caballero and Ceasar Torres,
and were all waiting impatiently for my report at a South Ferry
public phonebooth. Panamá was out on bail for being charged as

part of the radical underground independence organization Las Fuezas Armadas de Liberacion Nacional (FALN).

"Already?" was Panamá's initial response. Without waiting for further explanation, he added, "Okay, I'll go ahead with the press conference."

This was old Young Lords training. You always leave someone behind, in charge of calling a press conference to report on the demands of the offensive. The New York media swamped Battery Park to get the scoop.

Members of the media attempted to get to the Statue of Liberty, but were stopped in the South Ferry station by Coast Guard and federal agents. The government was rushing, too, and when the reporters arrived at the dock, the FBI's SWAT teams were already there. Only government officials were allowed to get near the Statue. Still, the media was able to take pictures with telephoto lenses of the huge Puerto Rican flag we'd placed on the Statue's crown. That was more than enough!

The restriction imposed by the federal agents was working to our advantage. All the reporters could do was take pictures of the only evidence that the statue was under control by our group, thus splashing front-page news all around the world with the image of the Puerto Rican flag waving freely on the forehead of the Statue of Liberty. Placed with so much love and compassion, it seemed to belong there. It gave a new and impassioned meaning to the words written for the Statue by Emma Lazarus: "Give me your tired, your poor / Your huddled masses yearning to breathe free / The wretched refuse of your teeming shore / Send these, the homeless, tempest-tost to me / I lift my lamp beside the golden door!" Just by flying our national flag on top of one of the most well known symbols of freedom, our entire operation was a success, regardless of what might happen to us afterward.

Panamá kept us informed, and we also had two transistor radios, one of them on WINS and the other on CBS. By noon, the seizure of the Statue was the lead story in the city, perhaps in the entire country. The radio was also providing us with important information on the movements of the FBI's SWAT team and other police forces to regain control of the Statue. Another benefit of the intense media coverage was that it served as a deterrent for any unwarranted violent action by the police teams. They had to proceed carefully because the public eye was on them. Both WINS and WCBS radio carried segments of Panamá's press conference in which he repeated over and over again that we were an "army" of unarmed individuals who had no intention in getting involved in any type of violent confrontation. We expected the culmination of our mission with the arrest of all the members.

At three in the afternoon, most of the Puerto Ricans among the twenty-eight had been complaining of being hungry and thirsty for a while. The situation was turning into a television sitcom, with people jokingly complaining that they wanted the authorities to come and get them before they died of thirst and starvation. The experience of most Puerto Rican members was that they would be arrested immediately after the action. Because of that, they had only brought something for breakfast, and a sandwich with a soda for lunch. After twelve hours inside the Statue during one of the phone calls from Panamá, we discussed an elaborate plan to rent a helicopter in order to make a food and water drop. It was ludicrous. I assured him that some folks from the Puerto Rican Solidarity Committee had brought enough nuts, raisins, crackers, and bottles of water for two days. We would all share.

After the ten P.M. radio reports, I realized this was to be a very long night. The seizure of the Statue of Liberty had become the lead story of the day, so I thought that nothing was going to stop the show or prevent it from being the lead story on the six P.M. television newscasts. I also guessed that the police forces would wait until deep into the night to make their move. During the long wait, I pictured in my mind the many Puerto Rican families who would watch the story while dining at home early that night. The broadcast in Puerto Rico would demonstrate again that Nuyoricans have Puerto Rico in our hearts. I even wondered if the nationalists in prison would get to see what we had done on their behalf.

By that night, we heard a radio report that the FBI's SWAT team had begun to mobilize to evict us by force. That could only mean one thing—they were prepared to use deadly force against us. What went through each person's mind? I can tell you that nobody expressed fear. Of course, there was no reason to dance, either.

Close to eighteen hours after the takeover, noises were heard outside, near the doors. The sounds were very distinct, very clear, as the FBI agents and other forces began the process of forcing their entrance. We looked at each other with a sense of accomplishment—and some smiles—as the sound of iron bars, hammers, and other tools were heard at every entrance of the Statue, thus proving we had done a thorough job in securing the doors and windows. Now they would have to sweat.

As they struggled to get in, we began to sing, in English and Spanish, revolutionary songs. The noises of the tools as they hacked at the doors and broke the glass mixed with our voices.

Just before they came in, I told my comrades to walk to the center of the circular base where we were assembled. We lined up, double file. No sooner had we formed the lines than uniformed men in full riot gear with automatic weapons and rifles drawn, rushed toward us. It takes only a minor mistake, any small stupid act, to turn such a situation into a bloody confrontation. We did not move. We were clearly unarmed. Still, they kept pointing the automatic weapons at us. Noting who was obviously in charge of the operation, I went up to him.

"My name is Mickey Melendez," I said. "I'm the spokesperson for this group. We're here to cooperate with you."

The man was tall, very strong, and looked like a no-nonsense type of individual, ready to pull the trigger of his automatic weapon at the slightest provocation. His densely blue eyes never looked straight at me. I noticed no fear or sense of intimidation in anyone among us.

"Everyone has instructions to cooperate," I insisted. "Just let us know what you want us to do."

Without a word, the officer in charge signaled his troops to go ahead with their plan. They proceeded to line us up: women on one side, men on the other. We were body-searched, stripped down to pants and T-shirts. They rummaged around every piece of clothing. Then they handcuffed us behind our backs with plastic handcuffs, and in a few minutes we were taken six at a time to a very small ferry—a tugboat, in fact—to start the trip back to Manhattan. They did everything in a hurry. Once we landed, we were instructed to climb into the Metropolitan Correctional Facility paddy wagons and the vehicles rushed to the Lower Manhattan federal prison. At one in the morning, there were over 100 people at the prison to greet us. As the demonstrators hassled the cops, we were escorted into the prison. We were so tired, that as soon as we were booked and given a cot, we fell asleep. Early in the morning we were taken to the courthouse on Lafayette Street and charged with trespassing on a federal facility.

When we arrived at the courthouse, Panamá had arranged

for prominent lawyers Michael Kennedy and the late William Kunstler to represent us. It was great political theatrics. I was sure that at the White House, President Jimmy Carter was doing much more than paying just casual attention to this case. In the end, we wound up having to pay $100 each for our "crime." It was a lenient sentence, but still amounted to $2,800. That sum was not easy to collect in those years, and we were forced to put our ingenuity into action in order to keep our collective asses out of jail. We had thirty days to come up with the money. The solution, however, came from an unexpected source.

The day after the fines were announced, bandleader Eddie Palmieri called Yoruba, now a television reporter. Palmieri wanted us to know that he was willing to donate the services of his band as a fundraiser to pay for our collective fines.

"The money," said the prominent Puerto Rican musician, "will be to pay for their fines. I am at your disposal."

Yoruba called me and put me in touch with the Palmieris. No matter who managed Eddie, the gig was always negotiated by Iráida, Mrs. Palmieri. Iráida and I spoke and she provided me with available dates. We came to terms quickly and a meeting was set up to meet with Eddie. After the usual introductions, Eddie wanted to know all the details and anecdotal stories of the Statue of Liberty takeover. I, on the other hand, wanted him to remember our first meeting on June 19, 1965, when I, personally, paid him for appearing along with Tito Puente at the Riverside Plaza hotel at one of the Plebeians' dances. I'm not sure if he really remembered me or just nodded to be polite.

We quickly organized a Statue of Liberty fundraising committee. I got in touch with Blanca Vázquez of Estudios Puerto-rriquenos at Hunter College and she secured the 2200-seat auditorium for us. We were looking for a bilingual MC who supported the unconditional release of the Nationalist political prisoners. I reached out to WKCR (Columbia University) disc jockey, Carlos de León and asked him if he would MC the fundraiser for the twenty-eight of us. Carlos was in the process of relocating to the West Coast and unfortunately couldn't be part of the event. Carlos assured me that he would find a suitable replacement. He called me back immediately. He had a friend who considered it an honor to MC the fundraiser for such a cause—Gerson Borrero.

We decided to charge $3 per ticket, a ridiculously low price, but we wanted a sellout. Bobby Rodríguez's band, known for their hit "Número Séis" (Number Six) which pays homage to the train that passes through El Barrio and the South Bronx, also volunteered to join Palmieri. It was a sold out show and we successfully raised the money to pay for everyone's fine. That night we raised something more than money. We were moved by the enthusiastic outpouring of support that we received from the community. It was a Young Lord moment—just how it was in the church, the truck, the hospitals and universities. "It was victory for all Puerto Ricans," proclaimed Gerson to the audience, as he brought the performers on and off the stage. The event was such an economic success, we convinced Palmieri and the band to go to jail with us, but not as inmates.

Palmieri had performed Sing-Sing with his brother Charlie years before. Eddie had done a lot of prison gigs here and in Puerto Rico. A few days later, we took Palmieri to entertain inmates at Riker's Island and Bedford Hills. That "prison tour" was meant to emphasize that people in prison have rights and deserve entertainment. It also reminded the government that the seizure of the Statue was done to pressure them to release the Puerto Rican patriots still incarcerated. I met some of the greatest musicians to ever play our music on that tour. Cachete Maldonado, Alfredo "Chocolate" Armenteros, Eddie Resto, and the great Puerto Rican percussionist Charlie Cotto, with whom I established a long-term relationship. He is a talented *timbalero*. He played with Richie Ray and Bobby Cruz in Puerto Rico for nine years, until Richie and Bobby became Born-Again Christian. They stopped playing for years until they were fully transformed and devoted their lives to the word of God. In 1977, Charlie was part of the rhythm section of the Eddie Palmieri Band along with Chucky López, Cachete, and Eddie Resto. Charlie had lost sight in one eye as a young boy. When I met Charlie backstage at Hunter College, it was clear to me that he had fallen prey to the white powder that gets cooked in a bottle cap, goes through a makeshift syringe and into your vein. By the time the needle comes out of your arm, you are free for the moment of life's pain. I knew Charlie by his reputation and recordings. When I met him, I saw a talented musician wasting his life away. I saw a human being in the depths of solitude. I could see myself in him. The love, the anger, the pain, the joy. One emotion replacing another instantaneously. At that very moment, I promised myself that he would not go to jail or be found overdosed under the stairs in the back of a building. Charlie trusted me enough to move him out of a furnished room that resembled a shooting gallery.

I took him home with me. We had an extra room where he lived with my family. Charlie began to believe in himself because he knew that we believed in him. The human, political, social, and economic transformations are endless when we believe in ourselves and others. Except for the musician community, Charlie's family and friends were all in Puerto Rico. My family became his family. With Madolyn Gonzalez, I baptized his son,

Carlito. Charlie returned to Puerto Rico with his wife Chari and kicked his heroin habit. He has been clean since. His three daughters, Chari, Milly, and Doris all call me *padrino*.

On September 9, 1979, twenty-three months after the Statue takeover, President Jimmy Carter signed the executive clemency order, granting each and every one of the Puerto Rican nationalist political prisoners unconditional freedom. Andrés Figueroa Cordero had been released due to deteriorating health in on Oct. 6, 1977, and died March 7, 1979. On Sept. 11 they were received in St. Paul the Apostle Church on 59th and Columbus Avenue. Their feet never touched the floor; the crowds carried them from the entrance to the altar. Lolita Lebrón, Rafael Cancel Miranda, Oscar Collazo, and Irvin Flores each spoke words of gratitude, encouragement, and determination. After all, they had been released on their own terms—unconditionally. For those of us that had been arrested, signed a petition, or gone to a demonstration, it was a chilling moment. Panamá presented the Puerto Rican flag that was placed on the crown of the Statue of Liberty to Lolita. The place roared. *"¡Viva Puerto Rico Libre!"* We could not have scripted a better ending. Lolita took the flag back to Puerto Rico and placed it at Don Pedro Albizu Campos's grave site.

Historians speak and write about the seizure of the Statue of Liberty as one of the key factors behind the release of the Puerto Rican nationalist political prisoners. Twenty-six years have passed since that glorious and historical moment, when Liberty wore red, white, and blue for Puerto Rico. That image will remain forever in the consciousness of every Puerto Rican, to be recalled instantaneously when our national dignity is threatened. The takeover of the Statue of Liberty on October 25, 1977 "had the thunder of the past, the fire of the present, and the wind of future."

SLEEPING WITH MY EYES OPEN

THE SEIZURE OF THE STATUE OF LIBERTY in 1977 and the release of the Puerto Rican political prisoners from federal prison in 1978 marked the end of an era in New York City's Puerto Rican activist politics. It was during that time that many Young Lords went back to our private lives and families. Some married and started to raise families, while others finished college and graduate school or developed careers in the media. A few never quite moved on and became walking shells—militants without an organization to fight with.

It was also a time to reflect, to look back at what had happened to the Young Lords and the organization's disintegration. It was the end of a particular involvement in politics for all of us. Soon thereafter, we began to see improvements that the

Young Lords had helped create. In the Bronx, for example, gringo politicians started to treat the Puerto Rican presence with a newfound respect, and in just a few months, the power of the Latino population's vote could not be ignored. There were those that understood, better than we, the fertile ground produced by the Young Lords. The movement paved the way for a new wave of Puerto Rican elected officials.

On July 2, 1979, after we had been separated for some time, Jennifer and I had our third child, Atariba Celia. She was named after my mother, and to honor Celia Sanchez, one of the two revolutionary women who had risked their lives next to Fidel Castro in Sierra Maestra. Jennifer and I had broken up mainly because of my indiscretions over the past ten years.

By 1980, a group of former Young Lords including Juan González, Richie Perez, and Panamá, held a convention in the South Bronx to establish the National Congress of Puerto Rican Rights, a grassroots human rights organization dedicated to securing full equality and an end to discrimination against Puerto Ricans.

Two years later, I became an intern at radio station WBAI with Alfredo Alvarado, who had a program on Saturdays from ten P.M. to twelve, called *Areito*, the Taíno word for "celebration." Alfredo was one of the first deejays to play contemporary Cuban music on the East Coast. Working with him brought me back to music, the one refuge I could always count on. In 1983 we went to the Vadadero Music Festival in Cuba, a five-day-long feast of Cuban and international music, featuring Oscar de León. Under President Jimmy Carter, America's relationship with Cuba had relaxed somewhat. Carter had established the "United States' Interest Office in Cuba" and Americans were not being harassed for visiting Cuba. It was my very first trip to this island and I was stunned at how immediately at home I felt. It was the same feeling I had gotten when I'd stepped off the plane on my first visit to Puerto Rico so many years ago. It is home where we are the majority, and in charge of the government. Alfredo also felt at home. I lost my radio partner shortly thereafter, when he decided to move to Texas.

I assumed that I was going to take over the radio show, but the BAI administration and management wanted to do something else. Out of the 168 hours every week that this public-access radio station broadcast, only two hours were aimed at the Puerto Rican/Latino community. Part of the reason management wanted me out, I believe, had to do with my history. The station didn't want me talking to a significant number of people via a radio show. They began to actively organize against me and eventually charged me with conducting an "unauthorized broadcast," and attempted to suspend my license. I was barred from the station. Management approached others, like musicologist Max Salazar, and deejays Jorge Quintana from Fordham University and Jose "Cheo" Diaz from Columbia University, to replace me. They even approached Felipe Luciano. No one stepped up because too many people in the business knew that I had paid my dues with Alfredo and deserved the position.

Eventually the station hired Nando Albvericci, who had been recommended by Henry Medina, and who owned Dick Ricardo Sugar's music collection. Sugar was the pioneer English-speaking deejay that introduced Latin music on the radio in the late '50s and '60s, and who was well known for being on the air after the famous Symphony Sid. Nando went on the air on November 17, 1984 (on my birthday, no less). After listening to his program, I was very impressed; he clearly knew our music. I hoped that Nando would be willing to listen to my side of the story despite what he may have heard from the station's management. I managed to get in touch with him through Felipe, and we set up a time to meet in person and talk. After we spoke, to his credit,

Nando decided to cancel his show. I had been in touch with a Chicano attorney at the FCC in Washington, D.C., and soon thereafter he informed BAI Management that they were out of compliance by not providing programming aimed at the Latino community in New York City, forcing the station to negotiate with us. Nando and I remained united and we proposed that the station allow us to do a show together. Nando's willingness to risk his show for me, impressed me greatly. People often define themselves in the heat of struggle. Nando had worked hard for years to get a program and took the chance of losing it after a short run. He believed in me, but most importantly, he believed in the power of our unified efforts—and we won. On September 21, 1985, we aired our first show, "Con Sabor Latino," featuring music and guests of importance to the Latino community. It went on regularly until 1995, two weeks short of our tenth anniversary.

During that time, we met almost every single artist in the industry. Our lineup of stars ranged from Eddie Palmieri, who became a regular on our show and appeared more times than anybody else, to Celia Cruz, Marc Anthony (when he was just starting off), and Gilberto Santa Rosa, before his very first album was released. We were very popular, especially when music giants like El Gran Combo, La Sonora Ponceña, Oscar de León, or Willie Colón would perform live in our studios during WBAI's famous fundraising marathons. It wasn't just the music community that supported us. One of the best fundraisers we ever had was when actor Jimmy Smits joined us on-air with his mother for a Mother's Day pledge drive.

Music was a large part of the program, but Nando and I also used the opportunity to discuss social, political, economic, and cultural issues. During the Gulf War, we invited people like Tom Soto, from the old Youth Against War and Fascism, Bronx congressman Jose Serrano, and Ricardo Alarcon—the highest-ranking delegate from Cuba in the United States at the time, and today the president of the National Assembly of Cuba—to discuss the war's legitimacy on the air. It was one of the most memorable shows that Nando and I hosted.

Meanwhile, at the premier club Ochentas, in Manhattan, I had met a woman named Millie Garcia who worked for Polygram Records. Our combined love of Latin music, plus her organizational skills and my experience producing music events, made us the perfect team and we started to discuss ideas for a show with Eddie Palmieri. Soon thereafter, we founded a production company called Nueva Vision. Our first production would be *Latin Pianos in Concert* under the musical direction of Eddie. We would place four pianos on one stage, surrounded by a band made up of some of the great musicians from New York and Puerto Rico. On March 17, 1985, the first *Latin Pianos in Concert* went on at Hunter College. We featured the late Charlie Palmieri and the late Argentine Jorge Dalto with Hilton Ruiz and Eddie. We then surrounded them with phenomenal musicians like Carlos "Patato" Valdez, Giovanni Higaldo (a teenager at the time), Dave Valentín, Ronnie Cuber, Sal Cuevas, the late Barry Rogers, and Jose Rodriguez, and my *compadre* Charlie Cotto.

The following year we took the show to Lehman College, where we sold out the Lehman Center for the Performing Arts—the first time for a Latino program. But by then, Jorge Dalto was ill and did not perform. Eddie dedicated a tango to his ailing friend. It also turned out to be one of Charlie Palmieri's last appearances before his untimely death. It was a fantastic production. We introduced Papo Luca and Michelle Camillo to a wide audience and brought back Hilton.

In 1986, I started to work with Ralph Mercado Management. I helped organize the annual Fall Salsa Festival at Madison

Square Garden. When I learned that Eddie Palmieri was having problems with his recording contract with Fania Records, I decided to negotiate with Ralph who would then speak to Fania and Eddie. I'm glad I did; it was the beginning of a successful working relationship. Ralph produced the last album that Eddie recorded for Fania and then the two of them began a new project together. The first album Ralph produced became a Grammy winner and his career took off.

In 1987, Nueva Vision organized a tribute for Israel "Cachao" Lopez, who is credited as the inventor of the mambo. A virtuoso bass player at a very young age, Lopez played with the Havana symphony and belonged to a family of accomplished musicians. He had also played with Tito Rodriguez for many years and recorded with Eddie Palmieri. Without a doubt he was a major figure in the development of Afro-Carribean music in the United States. Nando went out to Florida and found Israel working in a restaurant with a trio. He had not been in New York for ten years, when producer Rene Lopez brought him back to perform at Lincoln Center and record two albums. At the press party for the show, I was surprised to see my kids running toward me with a cake. Millie, now my wife (Eddie was our best man), and Artie Ramos, the owner of the Side Street club, had organized a party for me, and every major figure in the industry was there, including Tito, Cachao, Eddie, and Son Primero with Dave Valentín, who played two sets. It was a great feeling to be overwhelmed by the three hundred people who attended. I was elated.

I began to work for the Victims Service Agency (VSA) in 1987 with Dr. Ernesto Ferran (Ata's godfather), whom I had met when we were at Lincoln Hospital, and he was the only Latino medical student at Albert Einstein College of Medicine. Ernie was a board member with VSA and was able to recommend me for an interview for a full-time position. The agency helped provide safe housing and counseling for battered women, incest survivors, and others who had been violently traumatized.

Toward the end of my tenure with Victims Service Agency, in 1988–89, I began to work on David Dinkins' campaign for New York City mayor. My old friend Arnie Segarra was already in the thick of things. It was historic to help elect the first African-American mayor of New York City. Even though I suspected Dinkins was a typical clubhouse politician, he reached out to the activist community and very purposefully put together an activist coalition. Like many others, we worked hard for him. One time, someone commented to me and Panamá that we were "really good" when we were pro-something. Panamá turned to them and said, "We're even better when we're against something." When Dinkins got elected the activist coalition was credited for his victory. I was offered a position with the Health and Hospital Corporation. In this capacity I was able to institute acupuncture programs in every single municipal hospital, fulfilling a campaign promise.

During this time it became clear to me that in order to succeed in my field, I would have to get a postgraduate degree. I dreaded the idea of going back to school. I applied to Baruch College's Masters of Public Administration Program, only to receive a letter stating that I appeared to be a good candidate for graduate school—when I finished my undergraduate degree. As far as I was concerned, I *had* finished my degree at Westbury years before. Even though I hadn't gone through a ceremony, I thought I had completed enough credits to earn my degree but according to Westbury, I was six credits short. So not only was I *not* a college graduate, but I had been unknowingly lying about it on job applications for almost twenty years. I tried to negotiate with Westbury, but they wouldn't budge, and so I took two three-credit courses at Hostos Community College, transferred them to Westbury, and finally—after twenty-three years—graduated in June 1991 from the College of Politics, Economics, and Society. I started graduate school that September and graduated on schedule two years later. It was an exciting, but tumultuous time. I was starting a new job, but my marriage of five years to Millie was breaking up. This time it wasn't because of indiscretion. I just still had not learned how to be in a relationship.

While working at the Health and Hospital Corporation, and attending graduate school, I got a call from Alex Betancourt who told me that the New York City Housing Authority was looking for someone to direct their social and community services, and oversee a $30 million budget and over 1,600 employees. I got the job and worked under Sally Hernandez Piñero, the chairwoman specifically hired to clean up the agency's increasingly bad reputation. One of the most satisfying moments of my time there was when I visited the Hamilton Projects in uptown Manhattan to hear firsthand what residents wanted to see in their Community Center. At one point a woman who had lived in public housing for thirty-seven years stood up and said that this was the first time that "downtown came uptown" to ask for her input.

When Rudolph Guiliani was elected mayor, Piñero was out and Ruben Franco, Esquire, became one of five candidates for the chair. I spent a few hours briefing him on some of the current and pressing issues in public housing. He was eventually named chairman of the Housing Authority and shortly thereafter he fired me and one of my deputies, my good friend Tony Román. I was disappointed especially because Franco and Tony knew each other from Washington, D.C., where they both attended law school. Political allegiances got in the way of friendship. Tony and I sued the city and Franco for unlawful dismissal and defamation. They had us tied up in court for seven years, but we beat them at every appeal. We were ready to go to trial, and then the unexpected tragedy of September 11, 2001, occurred. The

Rudy Guiliani "halo effect" was part of the fallout; he could do no wrong. The city began to negotiate for a settlement and even though the offer was less than 15 percent of our original claim, we were advised to take it. We never had our day in court, but we were vindicated by the settlement.

In December 1998, I returned to Cuba after a long absence for the Havana Jazz Festival at the Téatro Nacional. Once there, I was again blown away by five days of wonderful and outrageous music. Five months later David Sanes-Rodriguez was killed, and I realized that I had been sleeping with my eyes open.

Epilogue

THE PAST IS NEITHER LONG NOR SHORT. It has no form. It is an invisible part of us, something intrinsic to our consciousness of being alive. Some of the people I have mentioned in these memoirs are already dead. Most are still alive. None, however, is the same person I've described here. My recollection of their deeds is just that—remembrances.

Sitting on the bench in the prison cell after the arrests in front of the United Nations, I was overwhelmed by thoughts of the past, especially those of the common past we all shared as freedom fighters. Eventually, my reverie was broken and sound turned back into sentences. I had reviewed my life and our story in the Puerto Rican movement. I looked around again and realized that I had a better understanding of all the people sharing those moments with me. Indeed, we were kids no more, no longer moved by radical theories, but still committed to peace, justice, and independence for our people.

For decades, Vieques has been a serious issue in need of a resolution. The thousands of Puerto Ricans living on that constantly bombed island only want to live in peace. They are not seeking a revolutionary change in the United States–Puerto Rico political relationship, they just want the navy attacks to stop. The damage to the environment and public health has been high. In Vieques, seventy-two percent of the people live below the poverty line. The rate of cancer is twenty-seven percent higher in Vieques than in the rest of Puerto Rico. Due to the bombing, the east coast of Vieques has more craters per kilometer than the moon. The overwhelming majority of Puerto Ricans on and outside of the island want the U.S. Navy out. Why is it difficult for the Navy to understand that it's wrong to poison the air and threaten the existence of so many people?

Since our first operation, other groups have formed and escalated our "civil (nonviolent) disobedience offensives." There are many heroes and heroines in this struggle. Many known, but many more remain unknown. On numerous occasions we have engaged in civil-disobedience actions in support of Vieques—at military bases, other government facilities, and ballparks. Members of the David Sanes-Rodriquez Brigade even went all the way to Vieques. Time and time again we have been arrested. At the Statue of Liberty, Panamá, Tito Cayak, Hector Matos, Ismarillis González, Camilla Gelpí, Mariana Reyes, Alba Noel, Olga San Miguel, Gazir Sued, Albanai Valentín, and Juan Casaña were taken into custody. It only strengthens our resolve. Every time it felt like a victory.

A few days after our arrest outside the U.N., groups supporting the struggle of Vieques began to think of alternative ways to protest publicly. Alberto de Jesús, also known as Tito Cayak, for example, managed to evade naval surveillance and was able to establish hidden quarters in a "military restricted area." He kept his lengthy protest in action until early June of 2000, when the Navy announced the resumption of the bombings. That prompted Ruben Berrios, president of the Puerto Rican Independence Party, to establish his own camp in the restricted zone. Those actions encouraged many to join the battle to force the Navy's aggression out of their territory. In fact, in a matter of a few weeks, the restricted area began to look more like a haven for protesters. At once, it became a mosaic of settlements, with many camps representing the various political, social, civic, and even religious institutions in Puerto Rico. This standoff lasted almost a year.

Placing themselves in the line of fire, Nestor De Jesus Guishard and Miguel Gonzalez formed a resistance group in Vieques, named MaPepe after two special people. Maria was the most beautiful and most requested prostitute at Pepe's brothel that primarily served U.S. Navy officers. However, she left to marry Pepe. When former clients asked to "visit" Maria, Pepe told them she was no longer working. Shortly thereafter, Pepe was found dead. No one ever stood trial for his murder. In the spirit of defiance and resistance, MaPepe has prevented numerous naval maneuvers and continues to gain strength.

For the first time since the battle had begun in the 1940s, Puerto Ricans raised a unified voice:

"United States Navy, Out of Vieques!"

Except for one very conspicuous dissenter: Then-Governor of Puerto Rico Pedro Rossello, an advocate of making Puerto Rico the fifty-first State of the Union, withdrew his support from the protestors. His opposition to the removal of the U.S. Navy from Vieques was probably one of the main reasons why his New

Progressive Party suffered a defeat in Puerto Rico's 2000 elections. Many pro-statehood advocates have remained supporters of Vieques, and Puerto Rico's senator, Norma Burgos, has been jailed twice for her defiant marches in the bombing areas. She joined more than a thousand who have been arrested in Vieques, including many labor and political leaders, as well as residents, workers and religious. Arrests and prison terms concerning Vieques have become an international shame. In the United States, the number of people risking their security and freedom has been overwhelming. Lawyer Robert Kennedy, Jr.; U.S. congresspersons Nydia Velazquez, Luis Gutierrez, and Jose Serrano; New York city councilman Jose Rivera; Dr. Steve Levine; actor Edward James Olmos; Local 1199 president Dennis Rivera; boxing champion Jose "Chegüí" Torres; Bronx borough president Adolfo Carrion; African-American activist the Reverend Al Sharpton; and, of course, our own Panamá—who has been arrested more than once.

Many public figures have signed petitions to the U.S. president, George W. Bush, asking him to order the Navy's immediate withdrawal from Vieques. They include the endorsement of two retired admirals, Eugene Carroll and John Shanahan, who have stated publicly that the use of the island for Navy bombing training is obsolete and adds nothing to our national security. All this led to President Bush's announcement in 2001 that "our friends and neighbors do not want us there," and that, because of it, the U.S. Navy would indeed vacate the island by May of 2003.

Once out, we should demand retribution and compensation for Vieques.

By the end of 2002, new defensive constructions were being developed in the area, and the bombings have increased. On Capitol Hill, congresspersons and senators known as naval advocates promise a tough battle if the president tries to push the Navy out of Vieques. As of this writing, the only meaningful actions taken by the Navy include more arrests, further sentencing of protesters, and the escalation of a violent offensive by Navy support groups. The New Progressive Party is harboring those groups that are threatening a renewed cycle of political violence in Puerto Rico. The situation is becoming increasingly volatile.

Fueled by the struggle of Vieques and the Navy's historical stubbornness and acts of insubordination, the Puerto Rican people are becoming increasingly nationalistic. It was only a few decades ago that it was considered a great honor for the island to become part of the U.S. Armed Forces, especially the Navy. Now, even the Fourth of July is celebrated with much-less-than-traditional enthusiasm. In 2002, news media polls in Puerto Rico showed that almost half its people did not see any reason to celebrate July 4th at all.

For nearly a century, Puerto Ricans were told that the United States wanted the advancement of democracy and the improvement of general welfare of the people. The U.S. Government was supposed to represent the rule of law, civil rights, and economic development. It was easy to foster a positive U.S. image in Puerto Rico with such benefits. We have been waiting for decades for "the liberty that was around the corner." The United States is not a freedom-loving nation for many of us, but rather a ruthless empire. The U.S. Congress has contributed to this by legislating a federal referendum for the people of Vieques to vote on the status of the bombings—Viequenses were offered $40 million to stop the protests now, and $50 million more if they vote "yes" on the Navy's continued occupation. The U.S. basically offered the people a $90 million bribe. The vote was taken in 2001 and the result was nearly 70 percent in support of the immediate withdrawal of the Navy. All people, particularly Puerto Ricans, should be proud of these brave Viequenses who were not willing to sell our national identity for millions. Isn't bravery the very foundation for democracy?

With each passing day it became more obvious that the Navy was supporting right-wing groups. During the Fourth of July ceremony of 2002, Rear Admiral Kevin Green, commander of the forces stationed on the island, attended the celebration supported by those groups instead of the official celebration of the state. The United States media has also backed off the Vieques issue, thus promoting further isolation of the Puerto Ricans in our demand for justice. Someday, the issue of Vieques will be solved. For the moment, the struggle continues. Things are still developing, and there is no way to know what the outcome will be. I am hopeful but very skeptical about "the rumors" that the Navy will finally leave in May 2003.

There is a new generation of young men and women with their own ideas and dreams. Many of them have been arrested defending Vieques. New issues, new struggles, new lives join the fight—it's an important component of the political life of the planet. The time will come when a new generation must take up the fight. For those of us who are rooted in the history of the late 1960s and early 1970s, we must support the new, young leadership of our movement. We still have a responsibility to-day—no matter what privileged position or material wealth. My story is the story of a group of young men and women who stood up together to meet the challenge of the times. As for many others, it began with a desire to reconnect with my roots (my history, my culture, and my past). It was this pursuit that gave me a sense of self and brought me to the realization that my life was part of a collective experience of a people, and that I have a responsibility to both my ancestors and generations to come.

Today, among former members of the Young Lords, there are many individual success stories, but of greater meaning is the success of the group. The numerous achievements of the Young Lords testify to the endless possibilities available when people use their individual abilities for collective action. We made the impossible seem possible. There is still much that needs to be done, and we need to organize, educate, mobilize, and agitate to make sure change happens.

Since my arrest in front of the United Nations building, many new people have joined our ranks. My enthusiasm and my strength have been renewed. Armed with the sincere belief that "our truth" will prevail, we are back on the streets.

Appendix

RULES OF DISCIPLINE OF THE YOUNG LORDS PARTY

Every member of the YOUNG LORDS PARTY must follow these rules. CENTRAL COMMITTEE members, CENTRAL and BRANCH staffs, including all captains, will enforce these rules.

Every member of the party must memorize these rules, and apply them daily. Any member found violating these rules is subject to suspension by the PARTY.

THE RULES ARE:

1. You are a YOUNG LORD 25 hours a day.
2. Any PARTY member busted on a jive tip which that member brought down on himself or others, can swim alone.
3. Any member found shooting drugs will be expelled.
4. No member may have any illegal drug in his or her possession or in their system while on duty. No one may get drunk on duty.
5. No member will violate rules relating to office work or general meetings of the PARTY ANYWHERE.
6. No one will point or fire a weapon of any kind unnecessarily or accidentally at anyone.
7. No member can join any army force other than the People's Army of Liberation.
8. No PARTY member will commit crimes against the people.
9. When arrested, YOUNG LORDS will give only name, address, and will sign nothing. Legal first aid must be understood by all members.
10. No member may speak in public unless authorized by the Central Committee or Central Staff.
11. The 13 Point Program must be memorized and the Platform must be understood by each member.
12. PARTY communications must be national and local.
13. No member may speak about another member unless he or she is present.
14. All PARTY business is to be kept within the PARTY.
15. All contradictions between members must be resolved at once.
16. Once a week all Chapters and Branches will conduct a criticism and self criticism session.
17. All members will relate to Chain of Command. Officers, cadre, and so on. The O.D. is the final authority in the office.
18. Each person will submit a daily report of work to the O.D.
19. Each YOUNG LORD must learn to operate and service weapons correctly.
20. All Leadership personnel who expel a member must submit this information, with photo, to the Editor of the newspaper, so that it

will be published in the paper, and known by all Chapters and Branches.

21. Political Education classes are mandatory for general membership.

22. All members must read at least one political book a month, and at least two hours a day on contemporary matters.

23. Only assigned PARTY personnel should be in the office each day. All others are to sell papers and do political work out in the community, including captains, section leaders, etc.

24. All Chapters must submit a weekly report in writing to National Headquarters.

25. All Branches must implement First Aid/Medical Cadres.

26. All Chapters and Branches must submit a weekly financial report to the Ministry of Finance.

27. No Chapter or Branch shall accept grants, poverty funds, money, or any aid from any government agency.

28. All Traitors, Provocateurs, and Agents will be subject to Revolutionary Justice.

29. At all times we keep a united front before all forms of the man. This is not true only among LORDS, but all Revolutionary Compañeros.

30. All Chapters must adhere to the policy and ideology put forth by the Central Committee of the YLP. Likewise, all members will know all information published by the PARTY.

THE YOUNG LORDS PARTY:
13-POINT PROGRAM AND PLATFORM
(OCTOBER 1969)

THE YOUNG LORDS PARTY IS A REVOLUTIONARY POLITICAL PARTY FIGHTING FOR THE LIBERATION OF ALL OPPRESSED PEOPLE

---

1. *We want self-determination for Puerto Ricans—Liberation of the Island and inside the United States.*

For 500 years, first spain and then united states have colonized our country. Billions of dollars in profits leave our country for the united states every year. In every way we are slaves of the gringo. We want liberation and the Power in the hands of the People, not Puerto Rican exploiters.

Que Viva Puerto Rico Libre!

2. We want self-determination for all Latinos.
Our Latin Brothers and Sisters, inside and outside the united states, are oppressed by amerikkkan business. The Chicano people built the Southwest, and we support their right to control their lives and their land. The people of Santo Domingo continue to fight against gringo domination and its puppet generals. The armed liberation struggles in Latin America are part of the war of Latinos against imperialism.

> Que Viva La Raza!

3. We want liberation of all third world people.
Just as Latins first slaved under spain and the yanquis, Black people, Indians, and Asians slaved to build the wealth of this country. For 400 years they have fought for freedom and dignity against racist Babylon (decadent empire). Third World people have led the fight for freedom. All the colored and oppressed peoples of the world are one nation under oppression.

> No Puerto Rican Is Free Until All People Are Free!

4. We are revolutionary nationalists and oppose racism.
The Latin, Black, Indian, and Asian people inside the u.s. are colonies fighting for liberation. We know that washington, wall street, and city hall will try to make our nationalism into racism; but Puerto Ricans are of all colors and we resist racism. Millions of poor white people are rising up to demand freedom and we support them. These are the ones in the u.s. that are stepped on by the rules and the government. We each organize our people, but our fights are against the same oppression and we will defeat it together.

> Power To All Oppressed People!

5. We want community control of our institutions and land.
We want control of our communities by our people and programs to guarantee that all institutions serve the needs of our people. People's control of police, health services, churches, schools, housing, transportation and welfare are needed. We want an end to attacks on our land

by urban removal, highway destruction, universities, and corporations.

Land Belongs To All The People!

6.   We want a true education of our Creole culture and Spanish language.
We must learn our history of fighting against cultural, as well as economic genocide by the yanqui. Revolutionary culture, culture of our people, is the only true teaching.

7.   We oppose capitalists and alliances with traitors.
Puerto Rican rulers, or puppets of the oppressor, do not help our people. They are paid by the system to lead our people down blind alleys, just like the thousands of poverty pimps who keep our communities peaceful for business, or the street workers who keep gangs divided and blowing each other away. We want a society where the people socialistically control their labor.

Venceremos!

8.   We oppose the Amerikkkan military.
We demand immediate withdrawal of u.s. military forces and bases from Puerto Rico, Vietnam, and all oppressed communities inside and outside the u.s. No Puerto Rican should serve in the u.s. army against his Brothers and Sisters, for the only true army of oppressed people is the people's army to fight all rulers.

U.S. Out Of Vietnam, Free Puerto Rico!

9.   We want freedom for all political prisoners.
We want all Puerto Ricans freed because they have been tried by the racist courts of the colonizers, and not by their own people and peers. We want all freedom fighters released from jail.

Free All Political Prisoners!

10.   We want equality for women. Machismo must be revolutionary . . . not oppressive.
Under capitalism, our women have been oppressed by both the society and our own men. The doctrine of machismo has been used by our men to take out their frustrations against their wives, sisters, mothers,

and children. Our men must support their women in their fight for economic and social equality, and must recognize that our women are equals in every way within the revolutionary ranks.

Forward, Sisters, In The Struggle!

11. We fight anti-communism with international unity.

Anyone who resists injustice is called a communist by "the man" and condemned. Our people are brainwashed by television, radio, newspapers, schools, and books to oppose people in other countries fighting for their freedom. No longer will our people believe attacks and slanders, because they have learned who the real enemy is and who their real friends are. We will defend our Brothers and Sisters around the world who fight for justice against the rich rulers of this country.

Viva Che!

12. We believe armed self-defense and armed struggle are the only means to liberation.

We are opposed to violence—the violence of hungry children, illiterate adults, diseased old people, and the violence of poverty and profit. We have asked, petitioned, gone to courts, demonstrated peacefully, and voted for politicians full of empty promises. But we still ain't free. The time has come to defend the lives of our people against repression and for revolutionary war against the businessman, politician, and police. When a government oppresses our people, we have the right to abolish it and create a new one.

Boricua Is Awake! All Pigs Beware!

13. We want a socialist society.

We want liberation, clothing, free food, education, health care, transportation, utilities, and employment for all. We want a society where the needs of our people come first, and where we give solidarity and aid to the peoples of the world, not oppression and racism.

Hasta La Victoria Siempre!

THE YOUNG LORDS PARTY:
13-POINT PROGRAM AND PLATFORM
(REVISED MAY 1970)

THE YOUNG LORDS PARTY IS A REVOLUTIONARY POLITICAL PARTY FIGHTING FOR THE LIBERATION OF ALL OPPRESSED PEOPLE

1. *We want self-determination for Puerto Ricans—Liberation of the Island and inside the United States.*

For 500 years, first spain and then united states have colonized our country. Billions of dollars in profits leave our country for the united states every year. In every way we are slaves of the gringo. We want liberation and the Power in the hands of the People, not Puerto Rican exploiters.

Que Viva Puerto Rico Libre!

2. We want self-determination for all Latinos.

Our Latin Brothers and Sisters, inside and outside the united states, are oppressed by amerikkkan business. The Chicano people built the Southwest, and we support their right to control their lives and their land. The people of Santo Domingo continue to fight against gringo domination and its puppet generals. The armed liberation struggles in Latin America are part of the war of Latinos against imperialism.

Que Viva La Raza!

3. We want liberation of all third world people.

Just as Latins first slaved under spain and the yanquis, Black people, Indians, and Asians slaved to build the wealth of this country. For 400 years they have fought for freedom and dignity against racist Babylon (decadent empire). Third World people have led the fight for freedom. All the colored and oppressed peoples of the world are one nation under oppression.

No Puerto Rican Is Free Until All People Are Free!

4. We are revolutionary nationalists and oppose racism.

The Latin, Black, Indian, and Asian people inside the u.s. are colonies fighting for liberation. We know that washington, wall street, and city hall will try to make our nationalism into racism; but Puerto Ricans are of all colors and we resist racism. Millions of poor white people are rising up to demand freedom and we support them. These are the ones in the u.s. that are stepped on by the rules and the government. We each organize our people, but our fights are against the same oppression and we will defeat it together.

Power To All Oppressed People!

5. We want equality for women. Down with machismo and male chauvinism.

Under capitalism, women have been oppressed by both society and our men. The doctrine of machismo has been used by men to take out their frustrations on wives, sisters, mothers, and children. Men must fight along with sisters in the struggle for economic and social equality and must recognize that sisters make up over half of the revolutionary army: sisters and brothers are equals fighting for our people.

Forward, Sisters, In The Struggle!

6. *We want community control of our institutions and land.*

We want control of our communities by our people and programs to guarantee that all institutions serve the needs of our people. People's control of police, health services, churches, schools, housing, transportation, and welfare are needed. We want an end to attacks on our land by urban removal, highway destruction, universities, and corporations.

Land Belongs To All the People!

7. *We want a true education of our Afro-Indio Culture and Spanish language.*

We must learn our long history of fighting against cultural, as well as economic genocide by the spaniards and now the yanquis. Revolutionary culture, culture of our people, is the only true teaching.

Jíbaro Sí, Yanqui no!

8. *We oppose capitalists and alliances with traitors.*

Puerto Rican rulers, or puppets of the oppressor, do not help our people. They are paid by the system to lead our people down blind alleys, just like the thousands of poverty pimps who keep our communities peaceful for business, or the street workers who keep gangs divided and blowing each other away. We want a society where the people socialistically control their labor.

Venceremos!

9. *We oppose the amerikkkan military.*

We demand immediate withdrawal of u.s. military forces and bases from Puerto Rico, Vietnam, and all oppressed communities inside and outside the u.s. No Puerto Rican should serve in the u.s. army against his Brothers and Sisters, for the only true army of oppressed people is the people's army to fight all rulers.

U.S. Out Of Vietnam, Free Puerto Rico Now!

10.   We want freedom for all political prisoners and prisoners of war.
No Puerto Rican should be in jail or prison, first because we are a nation, and amerikkka has no claims on us; second, because we have not been tried by our own people (peers). We also want all freedom fighters out of jail, since they are prisoners of the war for liberation.

Free All Political Prisoners and Prisoners of War!

11.   We are internationalists.
Our people are brainwashed by television, radio, newspapers, schools, and books to oppose people in other countries fighting for their freedom. No longer will we believe these lies, because we have learned who the real enemy is and who our real friends are. We will defend our sisters and brothers around the world who fight for justice and are against the rulers of this country.

Que Viva Che Guevara!

12.   We believe armed self-defense and armed struggle are the only means to liberation.
We are opposed to violence—the violence of hungry children, illiterate adults, diseased old people, and the violence of poverty and profit. We have asked, petitioned, gone to courts, demonstrated peacefully, and voted for politicians full of empty promises. But we still ain't free. the time has come to defend the lives of our people against repression and for revolutionary war against the businessman, politician, and police. When a government oppresses our people, we have the right to abolish it and create a new one.

Arm Ourselves To Defend Ourselves!

13.   We want a socialist society.
We want liberation, clothing, free food, education, health care, transportation, utilities, full employment, and peace. We want a society where the needs of our people come first, and where we give solidarity and aid to the peoples of the world, not oppression and racism.

Hasta La Victoria Siempre!

Acknowledgments

DESTINY OR ANSWERED PRAYERS, I first want to thank God, that spiritual force within each of us, for making all things possible, including this book. Over the last four years I have met some wonderful people who in their quiet support for this project, inspired and encouraged me. My inspiration came from two people and a book. Years before I even considered writing a book on the Young Lords, Ray Orta, who on occasion appeared with the doo-wop group the Eternals, would point an instructive index finger at me and say, "You should write the book on the Young Lords." For years he kept saying the same thing and for years I thought he was crazy until I read *Where White Men Fear to Tread: The Autobiography of Russell Means* with Marvin Wolf. In his book, Russell recalls the formation of the original rainbow coalition of the late sixties and mentions the Young Lords as a participating organization. The story of the Native people is told through the life of Russell and his role in the formation of the American Indian Movement. The Black Panther Party has three books telling their story. The struggle of La Raza on the West

Coast and in the Southwest is well documented. We have not yet written our story.

I want to thank Ray for putting the idea in my head—it traveled to my heart. This book is as much about pain and sorrow, struggle and hope, as it is about defeats and victories. Thanks to Russell Means and Marvin Wolf for giving meaning to Ray's words. A special thanks to Marvin Wolf for believing in this project from the beginning. Thanks, too, to Iris Morales, for her documentary on the Young Lords: *Palante Simpere Palante!* Her determination to overcome obstacles gave me the courage to be bold.

I am indebted to Artie Ramos, Alex Betancourt, and Ralph Mercado, who gave me a job when no one else would touch me. They allowed me to live with dignity.

Actor-comedian John Leguizamo and director John Cole (*Sex in the City, ER, Signs of Life*) quietly opened a door for me at the Jean Nagger Literary Agency; thank you both for your unselfishness. Thank you to our agent, Alice Tasman, whose persistent insight got us through the door—your devotion has not gone unnoticed.

I want to thank my cultural hero, seven-time Grammy Award–winner Eddie Palmieri, and all musicians for creating music. Your music is undoubtedly an "oxygen cocktail." Your music has always served as a refuge from pain and sadness; it has also celebrated our triumphs.

I am grateful for the friendship of Anthony Roman, Able Alverez, and Pastor Joseph Anthony Cortesi of Crossroads Tabernacle in the Bronx, you have enriched my soul.

There were many people who read drafts during this process and offered their comments. There are as many Young Lords' stories as there were Young Lords. Looking back, it was sometimes difficult to recall the sequences of events, places, times, and dates. If I spoke to three people, I had four versions of an event. This is what I saw and how I felt about it. I attempted to make this a collective experience. I want to extend deep appreciation to Iris Morales, Denise Oliver, Irma Iris Gonzales, Camila Gelpi, John Rodriguez, Jamie Rivera, Eddie Santiago, Maryann Feinburg, Marinieves Alba, Richie Rivera, Gloria Rodriguez, Gladys Peña, Luis Garden Acosta, and Dr. Steve Levine, a people's doctor. I am grateful to Johanna Fernandez Peña, Ph.D., our research assistant, for searching out details when my memory failed. *Muchas gracias* to Felix Rivera, Nilda Perez, and Jorge Matos of El Centro de Estudios Puertoriqueños at Hunter College; they always—miraculously—found the information for me. Thank you, Angelo Falcon from the Institute of Puerto Rican Policy, for your straightforward criticism early on.

I want to thank Felix Velasquez for his on-target criticisms of the early drafts. Thank you Roberto Sancho for your unwavering support. Also, Joe Conzo, Tito Puente's best friend, who has shared his collection for over forty years. Charlie Diaz, José Encarnacion, and Charlie Candelario of the 111th St. Boy's "old timers" for reuniting our people annually. I want to especially thank Elizabeth Pereira for offering her social, political, and cultural insights, always reaching to layers beyond the obvious. I want to thank you for your resiliency. Your contribution in drafting, with wisdom, the most personal and revealing aspects of my childhood was done with enormous sensitivity. I am eternally beholden to you.

Thank you Juan González for reviewing the manuscript. I appreciate your valuable suggestions and clarifications of places, dates, and times. I also want to thank Felipe Luciano for allowing me to quote from "Jibaro, My Pretty Nigger." I thank you both for our friendship.

Without the input of two more distinguished people, this would have been a very different book. There is no way to express in words or deeds the appreciation and admiration I have for Jesús Davíla and Vicente "Panamá" Alba. Jesús, who lives in Puerto Rico and is a brilliant journalist, on several occasions came to New York and spent many hours and days with us writing, reviewing, and editing. He simply gave himself and shared our enthusiasm and my Havana Club. *Compay* Panamá actually lived with me for three weekends, nine days, and dedicated himself to the book. I did the cooking. We stayed up with Cuban coffee. His memories of events are vivid and unpretentious.

I am deeply grateful for the photographs from Michael Abramson, Calixto Alvaréz, George Caver, and José Rosario from *El Diario/la prensa*. I am particularly obliged to Hiram Maristany who followed the Young Lords daily with an incredible eye and his camera. He has been documenting the daily lives of our people for over three decades.

My special thanks to Gerson Borrero editor-in-chief of *El Diario/la prensa*, for his cooperation in the making of this book. *Gracia Amigo.*

Many thanks to Julia Pastore, our editor at St. Martin's Press, who guided us through every step of the process. Her commitment to detail forced us to finally meet deadlines. Her flexibility allowed us to take a breath. Her insightful edits always added and expanded the story with color and sound. A heartfelt thank you.

My special thanks to Jose "Chegüí" Torres and his wife, Ramona. Chegüí is truly a champion, not just in the ring but also in life. I could not have written this book without him. This project has been a labor of love for both of us. In four years we shared our moments of tension and anxiety, of relief and joy. I knew I

was part of the family when, in the middle of working with Chegüí, he would take a blood-sugar reading and inject his insulin
in front of me. Thank you—*gracias un million*.

To all the political prisoners held in U.S. jails, thank you for
your example of valor. We demand your freedom.

I am a traveling man going east looking for work and light.
I want to thank all those people who brought light into my life.
You don't get to be my age and not have some regrets. "May no
one be less good for having come within my influence. No one
less pure, less true, less kind, less noble, for having been a fellow-
traveler in our journey towards . . ." I thank you for your interest.

Index